The Essence of Humanity

A Theory on the Origin of Religions and Reading of Sacred Texts

By

Moritz Bilagher

The Essence of Humanity: A Theory on the Origin of Religions and Reading of Sacred Texts

By Moritz Bilagher

This book first published 2024

Ethics International Press Ltd, UK

British Library Cataloguing in Publication Data

A catalogue record for this book is available from the British Library

Copyright © 2024 by Moritz Bilagher

All rights for this book reserved. No part of this book may be reproduced, stored in a retrieval system, or transmitted, in any form or by any means, electronic, mechanical photocopying, recording or otherwise, without the prior permission of the copyright owner.

Hardback ISBN: 978-1-80441-908-3

ebook ISBN: 978-1-80441-909-0

Table of Contents

Introduction vii

Chapter 1: Setting the terms 1

    Two worlds 1

    The mystery of phenomenology 6

Chapter 2: Factors determining the position of religion in present-day Western society 13

    Science, religion and sources of authority 13

    The appearance of Islam 22

    The philosophical objections against religion and their refutation: New atheism 32

Chapter 3: The theory of two times: Truth and the structure of the mind 42

    The architecture of perception 42

    The realm of the Prophets and the specificities of time 58

    The rethinking of religion 66

Chapter 4: Applications of the theory of two times 74

    Life and death: existence and essence (1) 74

    Utopias and ethics: myths of the end (2) 83

    Human in exile: the origin, paradise and evil (3) 92

    Time and the other: stories of creation (4) 99

    The gendered body: encounter of spirit, angel and animal (5). 108

    War and identity (6) 114

    Animals and food (7) 126

Chapter 5: Final reflections 130
    The land of two times 130
    The intuition of the arts 138
    Back to self: transcending identities 146
Bibliography 153

Introduction

The phenomenon of religion is in an interesting phase of its history of development: while most non-Western countries, with the notable exception of China, have often either large populations that identify as religious, are becoming increasingly religious, or both, so-called Western countries seem to be, on the whole, secularising, possibly with the exception of the United States. And even though religion is not necessarily the same as spirituality, it is almost as if, as the anthropologist Anil Ramdas once suggested, in Western societies, rationality has taken the place of spirituality (1993, p. 7). In the past, societies often represented phenomena of nature, on which people's lives depended, as human-like shapes that they turned into deities for them to converse with and obtain favours from (Freud argued that religion is an illusion born from human helplessness against nature, 1927/1961, p. 19). Many ancient Greek, Germanic, Nordic, Japanese Shinto and even Hindu deities reflect aspects of nature, for example Zeus, lightning, Thor, thunder and Fūjin, the wind.

If this interpretation of nature indeed explains the origins of deities, then it may be correct to imagine that, if that nature is subsequently increasingly understood through the (natural) sciences, it is demystified, and deities are no longer needed. Moreover, if the rational Western mind, which has lost the ability to recognise deities in nature and uses its understanding of nature to develop technologies to control it (nature), the relation between human beings and nature transforms to an even greater extent. The availability of technology, allowing for control through the manipulation of nature, tips the scale of the power relation between human beings and nature – at least seemingly and temporarily – in favour of the human being. In summary, the demystification of nature through the sciences, and its subjugation through technology, jointly imply, first, a demystification and, then, a subjugation of the gods.

From this point of view, it seems logical that scientific-technological societies tend to be more secular or, as per Ramdas, more rational and less spiritual than other societies. This seems indeed to be the case. Not only do statistics indicate a consistent decrease of formal adherence to religion among the majorities in Western countries, but it also seems that an increasing number of people in many Western societies believe that what religions tend to say is simply not true: that there is a Deity, that there is a super-natural reality and an inherent meaning and sense to life. As in the case of Freud, religion is explained as a psychological fiction or something else entirely: Durkheim, for example, argued it is society (1912/2008). In any case, it is a misunderstanding. While there may exist a desire for spirituality, reflected, for example, in the popularity of yoga, meditation and the renaissance of pilgrimage, the metaphysical questions connected with religious beliefs seem largely answered by knowledge from the natural sciences: there is a universe, but without a Deity in it; nature is ultimate reality, mysterious yet knowable; and there is no inherent meaning to life, as existentialist philosopher Sartre (1946/1996, p. 30) had already said around 80 years ago; there is only the meaning that we, human beings, attribute to it.

Yet, I offer this text with the argument that these are incorrect views. I argue that a Deity does exist, that there certainly is a super-natural (or rather, metaphysical) reality and that there also is an inherent, albeit not directly knowable, meaning to life. As I finalised this text, based on close to 20 years of research in the fields of (mainly) philosophy, religion, anthropology and psychology, reflecting and writing (not always in this sequence), I believe I have been able to formulate a philosophical theory positing that our human identity is rooted, in part, in a super-natural reality, where 'natural' is understood as physical or all that can be ascertained empirically. This theory takes human perception and, with greater precision, the mind as the source of perception as a starting point, applying psychoanalytical theory to arrive at the thought that, while the mind has a part that lives 'in time', i.e. consciousness, there is another part that is furthest removed from consciousness and therefore, in routine life, invisible, but eternal.

My idea is, fundamentally, that we, human beings, live in two worlds or 'times': firstly, direct time, of consciousness, which corresponds with the here and now. This is a world in which scientific laws hold true. But we also exist, through our minds, in another reality, which is mainly unconscious, where time, logic and causality play a much more relative role – that which Australian aboriginals, for example, have called Dreamtime. Our conception of Deity is at the root of Dreamtime, and the co-existence of this with our day-to-day experience of reality creates a specific tension that, if not subdued via stimuli such as those provided by the mass media, social media or other ways, demands a resolution. This tension, this irreconcilable 'error' woven into our beings, is the real root of religion. Religion, and the stories religion tells, is – are - the institutional resolution of the tension created by the co-existence in us of direct time and Dreamtime.

Before embarking further on this voyage, and explaining this theory in greater detail, I should clarify that I am familiar with the requirements for scientific theories and first and foremost Popper's principle of demarcation, based on the falsifiability of such theories. However, and as I will discuss later on, Popper clarified that this is relevant to theories pertaining to the empirically observable. Does this mean that nothing 'scientific' can be said about that which is not empirically observable? Not quite, even according to Popper; but for metaphysics, he defined other criteria, such as problem-solving ability. While I do not consider my theory to be within the realm of the sciences in the Anglo-Saxon sense of the word, i.e. the natural or empirical sciences, I will argue that it solves a great number of problems in understanding both what is true about religion as a generic phenomenon and what is true in religion(s), that is to say, specific instances of this phenomenon.

With this, I am looking to address two issues: first, to contribute to an understanding of ourselves, as human beings rooted in a spiritual reality as opposed to having bare existence. In this regard, this is a mission to help individuals understand their place in the world to a greater extent. In relation to Ramdas' idea that rationality replaced spirituality, mainly in the Western world, it seems that the relation between science and religion negatively affected religion as well as spirituality. This originates in an antagonism which existed between these two realms at least since Galilei's condemnation by the Catholic Church and reached its apotheosis with Charles Darwin's theory of evolution (1859). It destroyed, as many authors argued, the last bastion of the Church's claims to scientific truth. Nietzsche has, subsequently, among others, expressed the void this revealed. I believe this makes human life poorer and, in particular, people less able to face existential questions on life, death and meaning. Nevertheless, since then, some scientists sought to deal religion a final blow, rather than only criticise its scientific claims. In this context, I agree with the Carmelite nun and philosopher Edith Stein, born in Germany in the late 19th century and murdered in 1942:[1] in her view, there are three ways to the transcendent sphere: mystical contemplation, faith and reasoning (2009, p. 22). In this work, I follow the way of reasoning.

But I also have an intention that is more relevant to our collective existence, related to what Huntington (1993) called a clash of civilisations and, in particular, a confrontation between a certain type of political Islam, Judaism and, to an extent, Christianity and the Western World. While Huntington's thesis that the current main source of conflict in the world is the difference between civilisations (rather than, say, social classes), has been contested, it seems quite certain that, for example, the political reality of the existence of the State of Israel is largely based on the acceptance of its religious legitimacy in Judaism. This view is not shared by Islam or (all of) Christianity. The protracted conflicts that this difference in views seems to have given rise to may be compared with the Thirty Years' War: a very violent conflict in the 17th century, rooted in different perceptions of ultimate truth between Catholics and Protestants in Europe. According to Stephen Toulmin (1990), Descartes' principle ('I think therefore I am') was, fundamentally, formulated in reaction to this war. Descartes sought to devise a philosophical system based on purely mathematical truths that could be accessible to people of all denominations. He had argued that, if representatives of different religions could agree on basic truths, they could find a way to communicate and, in this way, similar wars could, in the future, be avoided.

---

[1] Stein included a section on 'Time and eternity' (p. 201) in her work 'Potency and act' (2009).

With no pretention to compare myself to one of Europe's most famous philosophers, what I intend to do is similar to this mission. However ambitious, I hope and intend to demonstrate that my theory of existence in two times may help analyse and clarify claims and stories from various religions, including Christianity, Judaism and Islam. In as far as religion refers to a human encounter with that which is greater than us, it can and must be considered a cultural phenomenon. Saying that one's religion is inferior to another one's is, then, similar to saying that their culture is inferior – something that, from the perspectives of cultural relativism and universalism (with which I mean here the fundamental equivalence of all cultures) is hardly acceptable. This is not to say that every religion is entirely 'true'; it seems fair to say that there are conceptions in religions that seem based on misinterpretations. I intend to make some of these visible. However, in the same time, I intend to demonstrate deeper truths hidden under the symbolic formulations in Sacred Books. These may have some elements in common, i.e. they may be ecumenical. While an all-encompassing comparative study of world religions is beyond the scope of this modest work, in the present, it is my intention to discuss a 'deeper truth', that, I believe, underlies Hinduism, Judaism, Christianity, Islam and religion in general.

To proceed, firstly, I will in greater detail explain the parameters of my undertaking (Ch. 1); then discuss a number of factors affecting the current status of religion in the Western world (Ch. 2); subsequently, I will introduce my theory (Ch. 3), which I then apply to seven cases (Ch. 4) and, finally, close with three reflections hopefully relevant to the implications of this theory (Ch. 5).

As a technical note, my citations from the Qur'an are based on a translation by the Pakistan-based *Ahmadiyya* movement. In this translation, the opening formula of each Sura (*bism'Allah el rahman el raheem*), except for Sura At Tawbah, is counted as a separate aya or verse. This is not the use in most Arabic versions. Therefore the numbering of ayas can differ by one from other versions of the Qur'an.

Moritz Bilagher

1

Setting the terms

Two worlds

According to Richard Rorty, in 'Philosophy and the Mirror of Nature' (1980, p. 149), it is the tension between universals (or concepts, such as 'humanity') and particulars (specific instances of concepts, for example, a specific human being) that resulted in the 2,500 years of philosophy that we know today. With this, Rorty echoed Horkheimer and Adorno, who had argued in their 'Dialectics of Enlightenment' that philosophy is defined by the attempt to bridge the gap between perception and concept (1944/2007, p. 31) as well as Heidegger who, in 'Being and Time' had, earlier (1927/2006, p. 216), already asked: "is it not allowed to ask for the ontological relation between the material and the non-material? Is it a coincidence that no progress has been made on this question for over 2,000 years?"

This seeming duality between universals and particulars, concept and perception, and the material and non-material, was arguably first identified in Greek philosophy, for example by Plato, who in 'The Republic' identified two essentially different worlds: that of the empirical,[2] i.e. the material world of sensory experience in which we live what we could call our 'everyday lives', or the world of 'particulars', on the one hand; and a different, abstract, non-material or over- or beyond physical (that is to say, a metaphysical) world of concepts and ideas, of which the empirical world is only a reflection (4th century BCE/1995a), on the other hand. The idea of this duality is not only relevant to philosophy, religion or science, but also to everyday life: after all, there seems to be, in most of us, a deep-rooted intuition that this is a way in which

---

[2] The adjective empirical means related to sensory perception. Empirical reality is usually equated with tangible reality and opposed to abstract or conceptual reality.

we can order the world: in addition to the things that we can see, hear and touch, there are other 'things' that we cannot, at least not directly, perceive. That there are ideas, beliefs, opinions, atmospheres, energies, spirits that are the constituent parts of our realities.

This duality has led to significant tensions. For example, it has led to questions such as: where do these realities – the abstract and the concrete - connect with one another, if at all? How do the material and the immaterial relate? How is the concept or idea of a human being related to a specific instance of one? Without actual human beings, would the concept of human beings still exist? And, conversely, without this concept, would or could actual human beings exist at all? One well-known philosopher who provided an answer to these questions is the French 17th century thinker René Descartes, according to whom the point of connection between the material and the immaterial is found in the human body and, more exactly, in a gland in the brain (1633/1972, p. 86). In his view, the human body is understood as a locus where the physical body and a spirit, soul or mind are united. For Descartes, both thought (*res cogitans*) and matter (*res extensa*) are substances, although he considered them utterly irreconcilable to one another.

Naturally, Descartes' dualism, which follows from the irreconcilability of matter and thought or, alternatively, the empirical and conceptual, resulted in difficult questions in their own right. For example: if these substances are really not reconcilable to one another, then how can something physical (for example, the substance of alcohol in a glass of wine) induce a state of mind? And, conversely, how can a decision that is made in the mind lead to action in the physical world? In an attempt to reconcile the tensions of Descartes' dualism, broadly two groups of answers have been given to Rorty's, Horkheimer and Adorno's and Heidegger's central question: so-called materialist answers, which understand the immaterial world to originate in the material world; and idealist answers, which understand the material world to originate, fundamentally, in the ideal, non-material, world.[3]

---

[3] According to Edith Stein, matter is that which is passive, while mind – or spirit – is that which is active (2009, p. 102, see also p. 111).

knowledge from pseudo-science: if something is scientific, it can, potentially, be falsified. If it cannot, it may still be true, but is not scientific. And, as Popper indicated, falsification can only be based on empirical observation. For this reason, to him, metaphysics were by definition unscientific (incidentally, as we shall see later, Popper made an allowance for the possibility that a metaphysical theory can be *true*). For Plato, such a clear division between metaphysics and science did probably not exist. To him, the metaphysical world was, above all, a world of unity; empirical reality, a world of multiplicity, or rather one of multiple appearances. For example, in as far as sensory perception goes, most of us would be able to see trees, being several objects in empirical reality. But the mind, which supplements the ability of observation, if it is not its source, can see unity or a common pattern in these objects, by means of which it can relate them, despite their differences in appearance and location, to one category: although one tree has leafs and the other one does not; although one is large and the other small; although one bears fruits while the other one has none – the intellect can identify all trees as belonging to this single grouping that we refer to as trees.

In Plato's view, the world from which the grouping or concept of a tree originates was the real world in that it contains the pure forms of objects that can be encountered in their various forms, but never in perfection, in the physical world. The idea that only in the conceptual world we can find the pure form of a tree implies that instances of trees, in empirical reality, never entirely correspond to the original archetype or *Urform* and are only derivates and therefore but appearances. The allegory of the cave illustrated this. Due to the combination of circumstances that, although the ideal world[4] is the real world, we seem mainly to inhabit the empirical world, for Plato, the main task of the philosopher is to look for unity in the multiple appearances of the empirical world. This meant searching for truth *per se*. For Popper, on the other hand, not philosophy but the empirical sciences represented the search for truth. In general, Popper would disagree with Plato on almost anything. For

---

[4] I refer to an ideal world in the context of a philosophical vocabulary, that is to say, I refer to an intangible world of ideas – as opposed to the material world - rather than a best possible world.

This difference in types of answers and, in essence, in understandings of the roots of reality is connected with a related question: if there really are two worlds (a material and an immaterial one), then which is the original one? The one we would understand to be the real world would probably be the one that we would consider to be the source or origin of the other one. To Plato, the more important of these two worlds was the metaphysical one. For him, the human condition implies an almost automatic misunderstanding of what reality is: surely, the way a human being is designed leads her or him to believe that the world of sensory perception is true reality. The fact that objects in the natural or empirical world can be seen, touched and sometimes heard, is evidence for the human being of its fundamental real-ness. Inversely, the intangible nature of ideas, notions and concepts leads human beings to believe that their existence cannot be proven, at least empirically, and that they are therefore not real. (Schopenhauer even said: "one could have the impression that our intellect is purposefully destined to tempt us into errors", 1818/1996, II, p. 208.)

Plato described the nature of what, according to him, is reality in his allegory of the cave (4th century BCE/1995a, pp. 170-174). According to this allegory, human beings are like creatures in a dark cave, who believe that the occasional shadows they see on the walls of that cave, falling in from the outside world, are reality. If these human beings were shown reality, that is to say if they would be led out of the cave, the light would be so strong that it might severely impair their vision. A diametrically opposed position, in the field of philosophy, was taken by the Austrian-English philosopher Sir Karl Popper, thousands of year later. Popper was, like Plato, a truly remarkable philosopher in that h covered both the fields of the philosophy of ultimate reality and wh we can know about it (in present-day language, he was a philosoph of science) and political philosophy. In the philosophy of science, developed a principle that has come to define an extremely imp tant division: that between scientific knowledge and pseudo-scie namely the principle of demarcation or *falsification principle* (1963/2

This principle says that it is straightforward to distinguish scie example, whereas for Plato truth was unchangeable, for Popper, truth was always tentative and subject to falsification. This by itself was not a new idea: the same was, in essence, already said by the 15th century Bishop Nicolas de Cusa who argued (1440/1954, p. 11) that: "our intellect, which is not the truth, never grasps the truth with such precision that it could not be comprehended with infinitely greater precision."

In 'The Open Society and its Enemies', possibly Popper's main work in the field of political philosophy, he called Plato along with Marx an enemy of the open society, because they were utopians (1945/2019) in two instances on this page. Utopia, for Popper, meant dictatorship. In 'Conjectures and Refutations', one of Popper's main works in the philosophy of science, he differentiated negative from positive epistemology. He understood positive epistemology as the optimistic belief that truth can be known and negative epistemology as the belief that it may exist but can, normally, not be known (1963/2006, p. 7). Popper, therefore, posited the falsification principle opposite the tyranny of the utopians: while the utopians, such as Marx, believed that they understood human nature, and consequently the ideal social order and therefore – borrowing from Hegel – the future of human organisation, that is to say socialism, and intended to efface all that stood between the now and the ultimate ideal, which would ultimately arrive in any case, through a revolution, Popper maintained that, ultimately, truth cannot be known and all we can say is that a theory to explain reality may, thus far, not have been falsified.[5]

One thing we can see clearly from both of these positions is that, while Plato is possibly the archetypical idealist, Popper is the archetypical materialist. It is not a coincidence that, while one took the existence of Deity for granted (4th century BCE/1995a), the other considered it unscientific, because unprovable and so, by extension, probably not true (1945/2019). In line with this, we see that the work of Plato was an almost direct influence on early Christianity (one only needs to compare 'Symposion' with the Letters to the Corinthians), while Popper

---

[5] Popper attributed the idea that choice of epistemology may have practical consequences to Bertrand Russell (1963/2006, p. 5).

was an important companion of scientific atheism in the Western world. Without taking any definition of Deity for granted *a priori*, if ultimate truth is not possible, then Deity may exist, but can probably not be known. If we ask which of these two positions - Popper's or Plato's – has the upper hand in most of the Western world today, it would probably be the former: the material world seems to be widely seen as the main source of acceptable knowledge (see, for example, Lewis, 1961, p. 135). It seems fair to say that (a) the increasingly broad acceptance of the empirical sciences as a source of truth and (b) a Popperian understanding of these sciences have had a hand in this. From this thought framework, the realm of the metaphysical is regarded with suspicion and, as Italian author Claudio Magris once wrote, the tangible world of phenomena, not that of introspection, reflection and the internal is seen as solid and, therefore, real (1998, p. 79; 2001b, p. 27).

This worldview, underpinning theories of what is true or even whether truth can be known at all, has important implications for our perceptions of reality. For one, it suggests that, in answer to an old ontological[6] question, essentially, mind is a product of matter. Therefore, the secret of what creates our perceptions, our values and self-awareness, must somehow be inherent in matter. But, in addition, it implies that Deity does not and even cannot exist, or at least not rest on scientific authority. In what follows, I will argue against this worldview; I will, consequently, argue that several of its tenets are probably not true and that Deity likely does exist before, one by one, discussing the main implications of this in our understandings of some main religious ideas.

The mystery of phenomenology

To start to illuminate the main questions raised in relation to the initial tension identified by Rorty, and consequently illuminate the nature and essence of this tension itself, I have placed it in the context of a wider dichotomy. The division in universals and particulars seems to run par-

---

[6] Ontology is the philosophical discipline dealing with the nature of reality, and in particular, the nature of the existence of things.

allel to other sets of tensions, such as that between abstract and concrete. The concrete is the world of sensory perception, in which the entities – or of which the component parts - are objects. The abstract is the world of ideas, of which the constitutive elements are concepts. To illustrate the distinction in and interaction between objects and concepts and by extension the abstract world and the concrete one, we could use the well-known example of a university.[7] If someone asked anyone else to show her or him a university, this other person could point to a building. However, even if this building were a university building, it is not itself the university. A university is not its lecture halls, laboratories, professors or documents constituting it – it is 'only' a concept, an idea people have, and mainly abstract.

The fact that a university is only a concept, and therefore immaterial, however, does of course not mean that it is meaningless or does not exist – on the contrary. An idea such as that of a university is one that can lead to an agreement to establish a range of physical realities, such as the construction of buildings, the recruitment of staff and the establishment of programmes of activities, including research. A university may, in this way, acquire a history and a reputation and begin to be seen as an actor as if it had its own will. I agree with the Turkish philosopher Ioanna Kuçuradi (2007) that "we need clear concepts", given that "[o]ne of the issues that philosophers are expected to deal with is the conceptual confusion prevailing in all areas of human endeavor [sic], but above all in political and semi-political discourse." In this vein, the division between the abstract and concrete seems at least to an extent related to the distinction in what in research methodology is called qualitative and quantitative research or what is in some environments called an interpretive paradigm respectively referred to as a positivist viewpoint.

I will not use these denotations any further, because I do not think they are very helpful. The oft-used differentiation, which roughly suggests that the first is related to words and the second to numbers, seems untenable. After all, words can be quantified and numbers related to a

---

[7] While I have searched for the source of this, I have not been able to locate it.

verbal reality. More plausibly, rather than two ways of telling a similar story, qualitative and quantitative research may represent two fundamentally different outlooks on reality: one that is subjective and one that is objective. The qualitative paradigm,[8] firstly, originated in the human or social sciences, where the founder of psychoanalysis Sigmund Freud developed interviewing techniques and where researchers such as Cushing and Malinowski developed protocols for observation in cultural anthropology (ethnography). Both these practices – psychoanalysis and ethnography – were developed in the late 19th and the early 20th century, as described by Michel Foucault in his *magnum opus* 'The order of things' (1966/2005).

The objectives of psychoanalysis and cultural anthropology seem to have been similar from the outset: to understand the way people make sense of the world rather than to understand how the world works objectively or independently of human perception. To illustrate this distinction, one could look at an object – say, a pen, book or bottle - and make a judgement on whether it is beautiful. When one examines whether this judgement is true, it will appear that this cannot be established, in as far as there is no universal standard for beauty. As Eco said in 'On beauty' (2010, p. 164), in the case of a judgement on beauty:

> ... both the intellect and reason give up the supremacy they respectively exercise in the cognitive and moral fields, and come into free play with the imaginative faculty, in accordance with the rules laid down by this last.

Whether an object is beautiful or not depends on the person or subject[9] – i.e. the proverbial 'eye of the beholder' – and is therefore subjective. As a consequence, asking someone whether an object is beautiful or not

---

[8] I am using the notion of paradigm here as defined by Thomas Kuhn ('The structure of scientific revolutions', 1970, p. 10), i.e. the whole of questions that defines the state of progress of any scientific discipline.

[9] In the philosophical vocabulary, a subject is someone who perceives something; an object that what is perceived. This should not be confused with the vocabulary of research methodology, where a subject is understood to be a subject of study, i.e. a participant in a research study who is in one way or another being studied (rather than studying).

will produce an answer that says more about the person than about the object.[10] It will help us understand the person rather than the pen, the book or the bottle (Bilagher, 2005), which in any event seems to be the main objective of the humanities *per se*. The fact that subjective reality refers, in the first place, to the subject (person) rather than the object (or thing) does however not mean that it is not real. The extent to which things are beautiful or not may be a very real component of one's being in the world and experience of things. Subjective perceptions are likely to influence people's actions, which can lead to effects in objective reality and the subjective experience of other persons than the immediate subject. It thus seems natural for the humanities, but also for the social sciences, to rely on methods, instruments and techniques of data collection that examine subjective perceptions rather than objective reality. To give one example, when I know the height, weight and colour of hair of a person, I cannot say that I know this person even though these data provide objective information about her or him. To get to know the person in question, that is to say, to get to know them as an individual and a human being would inevitably mean: getting to know her or him subjectively – to develop an understanding of what their opinions, thoughts, convictions and certainties are.

The roots of quantitative research, on the other hand, are firmly located in the natural sciences. They refer to the objective, empirical and tangible world (see Footnote 2); objective, in the sense that the characteristics of phenomena in this world are supposedly equal to everyone. If the person I mentioned above would weigh 80 kg, this should be so for everyone. It is not thinkable that according to one's correct measurement this person would weigh 80, and to someone else's 85 kg. Their weight is not subject to opinion but considered a matter of fact. The fact that the origins of the quantitative perspective are in the natural sciences does evidently not mean that it is not also applied in the social or human sciences. Given the association of the social and human sciences with the realm of subjectivity, this is usually done by

---

[10] Of course, when one examines perceptions of beauty on a larger scale, the results can tell us something about a culture or even humanity within a given timeframe.

operationalising concepts. This means developing indicators, or proxy measures for concepts that can themselves not be directly perceived and therefore measured. As such, indicators are objectively perceptible events or instances in empirical reality that indicate the presence or absence of a concept. For example, if a smile is taken to be an indication of the presence of happiness (itself a concept), and quantity – rather than duration or intensity – a yardstick of measure, then the number of times someone smiles in a given period can be seen as indicating one's happiness.

The above does not mean that the objective can simply be equated with the concrete, and the subjective with the abstract. The subjective dimension, as it appears in qualitative studies, is that of personal experience. Concepts, although, from a materialistic[11] perspective existing in the human mind alone, are not by definition or at all subjective. For example, although the university mentioned above is not a concrete or tangible entity (that is to say, it is not an object), its existence is an objective or at least inter-subjective[12] fact. Similarly, the existence (rather than the presence) of happiness according to given indicators is not a matter of view, perception or opinion, but established reality, albeit not material; although, again, as mentioned above, it is recognised that substances can change one's state of mind. There is, however, one sense in which it is true to think of subjective reality in alignment with conceptual reality: concepts do not exist out of the human mind. They cannot be observed directly in the natural world. Universities only manifest themselves materially because subjects (persons) are the carriers of that idea. As such, the abstract world may not be local, but its existence is still limited to where there are subjects or, in Kant's vocabulary, where there is *Vernunft* (reason).

This points to something important: the central role that the mind, the carrier of Vernunft or reason, plays in the worldviews I mentioned pre-

---

[11] In philosophy, and in the way I use the word in this work, materialism stands for the belief that matter is the source of reality, rather than mind; it is normally opposed to idealism, which holds the opposite.

[12] This denotes something that is real for more than one person.

viously. For example, in 'Philosophy and the mirror of nature', Rorty said that Kant had revealed that many of the questions that philosophy had faced in its 2,500 years of history are related to how the mind is set up and, therefore, the 'problems' it had created for itself, rather than to an intrinsic characteristic of nature or reality, independent of the human mind (1980, pp. 160-161). It seems that these questions are invoked by the virtually automatic misunderstanding of reality that is due to our human condition, as suggested by Plato and Schopenhauer.[13] In contemporary questions on how the mind can exist at all, we find new formulations of the old philosophical questions. A logical consequence of how the materialists intended to ground reality entirely in the empirical, and liberate it of metaphysics, subjectivity or phenomenology, appeared in the relatively new field of Consciousness Studies and artificial intelligence as a 'hard problem'. This hard problem, described by David Chalmers (1995, p. 200), refers to the issue that, while consciousness or artificial intelligence may be described from the outside, i.e. physically, a scientific description is insufficient to explain how observable processes create something from the inside, that is to say, the mentioned perception, subjectivity and phenomenology.

What science is mainly interested in, is the objective world, often without realising that it approaches this with what Kant called *a priori* knowledge, i.e. time, space and causality, which are all related to subjectivity or phenomenology. It increasingly asks itself where this comes from (and then, sometimes, answers, for example, that time does not exist). While a priori concepts are indeed abstract, and intangible, they are at the root of empirical reality. After all, empirical observations cannot take place outside of time or space. But time and space are, in the same time, the root of phenomenology, which is, by definition, subjective. The thought that underpins the theory which I will lay out is that Deity exists as the source or root of this (subjective) reality, not as its manifestation. Deity is the root abstract 'concept of concepts' ordering our nat-

---

[13] Incidentally, the similarities between Plato's and Kant's thoughts seem to be systematic rather than coincidental. For example, Kant's concept of the Ding an sich (thing in itself) seems similar to Plato's archetypal forms (Schopenhauer, 1818/1996, I, p. 247).

ural world. Deity is, roughly said, at the bottom of our consciousness or perception,[14] rather than a content of our consciousness, which is the reason that it can never be 'found' by natural scientists. It is co-constitutive of our identities, while, due to the set-up of our minds, having necessarily to be perceived as an Other to our minds. In what follows, I will explain in greater detail what this all means, as my argument unfolds, as well as demonstrate how my hypothesis can pass most tests, not of scientific verification, but of alignment with what we know about Deity from sacred texts and our understandings of it – and, also, to help us take a look at these in a new light.

While this underpinning thought is not exactly a proof in the classical, Popperian sense of the word, I would like to remind the reader that proof in this sense even according to Popper is only applicable to the world of the empirical. As to the realm of the metaphysical, Popper maintained that there are different possibilities to support the truth claim of statements: one of these is the ability to solve problems (1963/2006, p. 269). I assert that my solution does solve a great number of problems around the understanding of Deity, from the view that Deity is invisible to scientists (i.e. Deity is not empirical) to how religious texts explain Deity. How this works in different circumstances I will address in the following sections. First, however, I will discuss further some of the factors influencing the position of religion in contemporary society.

---

[14] I explained this in some detail in a separate article (Bilagher, 2010) and will explain it further in subsequent sections.

2

Factors determining the position of religion in present-day Western society

Science, religion and sources of authority

The main challenges to the existence of Deity, in any form, have in the past 500 years or so not come from philosophers like Popper. They arguably came from the natural sciences. From Copernicus' theory that the known universe (or what we now call the 'solar system') is heliocentric, contradicting the tenets of the Catholic Church of the time, and promoted around 100 years later, in the 1600s, by Galilei, to Darwin's theory of evolution in the 1850s, which challenged the Biblical myth of creation and, finally, Richard Dawkins' strong criticism of religion in general (2007), have a close relation with a growing secularisation of the general worldview over the past few hundred years.

At this point, the cosmopolitan reader will, likely, observe that the above seems to represent a conflict between *Western* religion, and in particular Christianity, with modern science, which is widely considered a Western development. This is a fair qualification. My focus is, for the moment, on Europe, where the relation between (revealed) religion and 'rational' or scientific reason has for a long time constituted a difficult question, with important implications not only for the worlds of theology and philosophy, but also for cultures and societies, including politics. However, the same can roughly be said about the Islamic-Arab world as well, where, as far back as the 12th century, the works of the Spanish-Arabic philosopher Averroes (*Ibn Rushd*) were burnt because of his assertion that religion and philosophy did not need to be in conflict with one another, but that, instead, "there was a harmony between faith and reason in Islam" (Goodman and Russell, 1991, p. 16).

However, with reference to religious, for example, Biblical stories like the myth of creation, not just the natural scientist but even the logical thinker could argue that a world could have not been created in any number of days before the sun and moon, which cause the very notions of night and day, had been created. This argument was put forward by the 17th and early 18th century British scientist Thomas Burnet (Kroonenberg, 2007, p. 56). Less well-known is that even St. Augustine had already mentioned this in 'The City of God', over a thousand years earlier (Augustinus, 426/2007, p. 503). In the view of St. Augustine, the reason for this apparent logical discrepancy is that, in regard to the story of creation, we have to think of time in different terms than one would in his, or our time; for St. Augustine, the real meaning of the word 'day' in the Bible is 'time' (426/2007, p. 989).

Indeed, such an argumentation as that of our logical thinker – and the idea that theories such as Darwin's invalidate the myth of creation – holds only in as far as Christianity does not reject an allegorical reading of the Christian sacred texts. In the Middle Ages, allegorical reading of the Bible was the norm, arguably as suggested in the Bible itself, for example in Galatians 4:24 (as per the Saint James translation: "Which things are an allegory: for these are the two covenants; the one from the mount Sinai, which gendereth to bondage, which is Agar"). For St. Augustine, a non-literal reading of the Bible was natural (426/2007, p. 762) yet, on the verge of the Middle Ages and the Renaissance, an epistemological shift[15] took place. Interestingly, this 'new' notion that the Bible is to be interpreted literally has itself made Christianity as a belief-system significantly more vulnerable, as 20th century theologian Tillich (1963, in Dobzhansky, 1969, p. 34) argued, when saying that: "The first step toward non-religion of the western world was made by religion itself. This was when it defended its great symbols, which were its means of interpreting the world and life, not as symbols, but as literal stories." The same, in essence, had already been said almost a 100 years earlier, by the 19th century German philosopher Friedrich Nietzsche, who argued, in his work 'The birth of tragedy' (1872/1953, p. 68):

---

[15] An epistemological shift is understood here as a shift in the understanding of a certain reality and how we can have knowledge of it.

2

Factors determining the position of religion in present-day Western society

Science, religion and sources of authority

The main challenges to the existence of Deity, in any form, have in the past 500 years or so not come from philosophers like Popper. They arguably came from the natural sciences. From Copernicus' theory that the known universe (or what we now call the 'solar system') is heliocentric, contradicting the tenets of the Catholic Church of the time, and promoted around 100 years later, in the 1600s, by Galilei, to Darwin's theory of evolution in the 1850s, which challenged the Biblical myth of creation and, finally, Richard Dawkins' strong criticism of religion in general (2007), have a close relation with a growing secularisation of the general worldview over the past few hundred years.

At this point, the cosmopolitan reader will, likely, observe that the above seems to represent a conflict between *Western* religion, and in particular Christianity, with modern science, which is widely considered a Western development. This is a fair qualification. My focus is, for the moment, on Europe, where the relation between (revealed) religion and 'rational' or scientific reason has for a long time constituted a difficult question, with important implications not only for the worlds of theology and philosophy, but also for cultures and societies, including politics. However, the same can roughly be said about the Islamic-Arab world as well, where, as far back as the 12th century, the works of the Spanish-Arabic philosopher Averroes (*Ibn Rushd*) were burnt because of his assertion that religion and philosophy did not need to be in conflict with one another, but that, instead, "there was a harmony between faith and reason in Islam" (Goodman and Russell, 1991, p. 16).

However, with reference to religious, for example, Biblical stories like the myth of creation, not just the natural scientist but even the logical thinker could argue that a world could have not been created in any number of days before the sun and moon, which cause the very notions of night and day, had been created. This argument was put forward by the 17th and early 18th century British scientist Thomas Burnet (Kroonenberg, 2007, p. 56). Less well-known is that even St. Augustine had already mentioned this in 'The City of God', over a thousand years earlier (Augustinus, 426/2007, p. 503). In the view of St. Augustine, the reason for this apparent logical discrepancy is that, in regard to the story of creation, we have to think of time in different terms than one would in his, or our time; for St. Augustine, the real meaning of the word 'day' in the Bible is 'time' (426/2007, p. 989).

Indeed, such an argumentation as that of our logical thinker – and the idea that theories such as Darwin's invalidate the myth of creation – holds only in as far as Christianity does not reject an allegorical reading of the Christian sacred texts. In the Middle Ages, allegorical reading of the Bible was the norm, arguably as suggested in the Bible itself, for example in Galatians 4:24 (as per the Saint James translation: "Which things are an allegory: for these are the two covenants; the one from the mount Sinai, which gendereth to bondage, which is Agar"). For St. Augustine, a non-literal reading of the Bible was natural (426/2007, p. 762) yet, on the verge of the Middle Ages and the Renaissance, an epistemological shift[15] took place. Interestingly, this 'new' notion that the Bible is to be interpreted literally has itself made Christianity as a belief-system significantly more vulnerable, as 20th century theologian Tillich (1963, in Dobzhansky, 1969, p. 34) argued, when saying that: "The first step toward non-religion of the western world was made by religion itself. This was when it defended its great symbols, which were its means of interpreting the world and life, not as symbols, but as literal stories." The same, in essence, had already been said almost a 100 years earlier, by the 19th century German philosopher Friedrich Nietzsche, who argued, in his work 'The birth of tragedy' (1872/1953, p. 68):

---

[15] An epistemological shift is understood here as a shift in the understanding of a certain reality and how we can have knowledge of it.

Denn dies ist die Art, wie Religionen abzusterben pflegen: wenn nämlich die mythischen Voraussetzungen einer Religion under den strengen, verstandesmäßigen Augen eines rechtgläubigen Dogmatismus als eine fertige Summe von historischen Ereignissen systematisiert werden und man anfängt, ängstlich die Glaubwürdigkeit der Mythen zu verteidigen, aber gegen jedes natürliche Weiterleben und Weiterwuchern derselben sich zu sträuben, wenn also das Gefühl für den Mythus abstirbt und an seine Stelle der Anspruch der Religion auf historische Grundlagen tritt.

Therefore, this is how religions tend to die off: when the mythical underpinnings of a religion are systematised under the rational supervision of a consequent dogmatism, as a ready sum of historical events, when one commences to fearfully defend the credibility of myths, but to act against any natural life and growth of the same, when, therefore, the feeling for myth dies off and, at its place, religion makes claim to historical truth.

Yet the mentioned epistemological shift is quite understandable. When the reformation movement began to challenge the Church, which had until then been the highest authority, it needed an even higher authority to refer to: the Bible. Therefore, to an extent, the mentioned shift was not just a shift between the Middle Ages and the renaissance but also, or rather, between Catholic Church and reformation. Protestantism rejected the Catholic tradition of allegory in favour of the notion of *sola scriptura*, i.e. that only the Bible is considered a source of theological knowledge among other factors in order to decrease the authority of the Latin-speaking Catholic clergy and empower readers of the Bible. While this led to translations of the Bible into various languages, it also led to a fixation on the Bible itself as a literal and not an allegorical text.

In the same 16th century as the one in which the reformation started, with the publication of Martin Luther's 95 theses in Wittenberg (1517), the Catholic Church was challenged from another angle. It seems rather certain that the struggle of the Church with science began with Copernicus' above-mentioned discovery that, in contradiction with both scientific and religious beliefs at the time, the earth revolves around the sun (1534). This, Goodman and Russell wrote (1991, p. 66), was a view that would destroy the newly developed synthesis between religious tenets and (Aristotelian) philosophy, scholasticism; something that the establishments – both Protestant and Catholic – would not accept without resistance. It is understandable that the prestige of the Church was to a large extent based on the perception that it had expert 'cosmological' knowledge, that is to say, knowledge of the ultimate order of things. Therefore, if the Church would admit that their worldview had been mistaken on one account, on how many other accounts could it have been mistaken? After all, Copernicus' theory seemed to contradict at least one passage of the Bible, namely Joshua 10:12-14. What could this mean for its position? It is hard, Goodman and Russell find, in relation to this affair, "to avoid the cynical view of historical conflicts that they are rarely about principles, but nearly always about power" (ibid.).

There are some parallels between this and a similar history in the Arab Muslim world. As briefly alluded to earlier, in this cultural realm as well, (scientific) reason had been contrasted with revelation. Either idea – that reason was superior to revelation or that revelation was superior to reason – was represented in a school: in Baghdad, in the 8th century, a university was founded with the name House of Wisdom (Dar al Hikmah). This was associated with the rationalist school of the Muta'zilin, which fostered great scientific advances in the Islamic world. In the 10th century, however, the anti-rationalist school of the Ash'ari emerged, which considered the rationalists a threat to Islam. Consequently, this school and, in particular, the philosopher Al Ghazali engaged in battle with the Muta'zilin and, ultimately, towards the end of 14th century, emerged victorious. Both schools could sustain their arguments with references to Islam's main sacred text, the Qur'an. The notion of the primacy of revelation over reason seems supported by some verses (Ayas), which say, for example, that posing too many questions can lead to unbelief (Sura Al Maidah 5, Ayas 102 – 104). Parallel to this, however, exists the claim that there is no inherent contradiction between Islam and scientific advancement. According to the foreword to the Qur'an of the Ahmadiyya movement (1994, p. 166), Islam and the revelation of the Qur'an are aligned with scientific advances such as evolution theory. An oft-cited example in this regard is the Aya describing the development of the human foetus (Sura Al Mominoen 23, Aya 15).

The literal reading of the Bible, and the authority with which this source was endowed, implied a separation of reason and science: reason was adapted to the prevailing doctrine and scientific exploration allowed in as far as it would not contradict it. In a way, this suggested that truth could only be found through deduction,[16] where the primary premise would be the truth of the Bible. In light of the importance of the deductive style in Greek philosophy, it is not surprising that, in the later Middle Ages, Aristotle became the philosopher of the Church (a synthesis of the theological and philosophical theses of the Church and Aristotle was achieved by Thomas Aquinas); earlier on, Plato had had a greater influence, for example on St. Augustine and, incidentally, according to Goodman and Russell, also "[f]or some Muslims the logic and reasoning of Aristotle was seen as a valuable tool to defend the basic tenets of Islam" (1991, p. 16).

It is probably not surprising that the Church, which had united with and grown into a worldly power after becoming the *de facto* religion of state of the Roman Empire in 380, would not look kindly at the scientific method if it were a competitor for power. While this alone would be enough to explain the discord that Goodman and Russell described, which occurred in the late 16th and early 17th century (around the beginning of what is referred to as the scientific revolution), part of this hostility was also based on the fact that, in that time, experimental science had a clear link to what was considered 'magic' (alchemism, the quest for the philosopher's stone, Hermetism) and was therefore thought of as impure. Interestingly, some authors, such as Frances Yates, saw this "active, magical, manipulative approach of nature as the principal cause of the Scientific Revolution", as Goodman and Russell (1991, p.

---

[16] In the vocabulary of the philosophy of science, deduction is contrasted with induction. Deduction stands for inferring specific statements from general statements, whereas induction stands for inferring general rules from specific observations.

28) assert. In spite of this, a remainder of a split between 'official science' and alternative science can still be recognised in the medical sciences, nowadays, where the official medical sciences, or allopathic medicine, are contrasted with alternative medical methods, such as acupuncture, phyto-therapy and homeotherapy.

The pressure on the Church, which had already been struggling because of the Protestant secession, and which itself launched a Counterreformation, increased when, in Italy, Copernicanism was revived by the Tuscan astronomer Galileo Galilei. The world picture of the Catholic Church was at stake and, as mentioned, along with that, its claim to power. As a consequence, Galilei was declared more dangerous than Luther or Calvin (id., p. 112). Be that as it may, with growing empirical evidence in support of Copernicanism, the position of the Church was bound to become ultimately untenable (although, as Goodman and Russell said, in Portugal, Copernicanism was not fully accepted until as late as the 18th century,[17] 1991, p. 127). To reconcile Copernicus' position with the perceived needs of the Church, in 1623, Galileo introduced the concept of the 'Book of Nature', which was meant to stand next to the Bible and of which the subject was to be what is scientifically true (or real). In contrast, the Bible was understood to address what is morally true (or good). Where the Bible, the Book of the Creator, was written by the ancient Prophets, the Book of Nature, that is, the book of Creation, would have to be written by scientists.

Incidentally, the concept of the Book of Nature had already existed before Galileo, in Christian thought. However, at the time, it stood for something else: the idea that nature was filled with signs from the Creator that could be interpreted via the scriptures (the Bible). The fact that, in Galileo's interpretation, human beings (or rather scientists and not prophets) would become the writers of this Book of Nature was something the Church could not accept. While Galileo's Book of Nature would still accept the concept of a 'creation created by a Creator', what would the Church think of a creation (i.e. nature) that was its own Creator? According to Toulmin and Goodfield (1982, p. 163), the

---

[17] See also Hooykaas, 1973, p. 58, in: Goodman & Russell, 1991, p. 63.

last drop contesting the scientific authority of the Bible was Darwin's theory of evolution of 1859, according to which the human species was not directly created by a Divine Creator, but through a process of chance called 'natural selection'. Darwin himself became quite critical of religion in his later life, eventually comparing the urge to believe in a Creator to a remnant of an atavistic instinct, such as the hate of a monkey towards a snake, principally based on fear, in his autobiography (1958, p. 93). It should be noted that this idea was omitted from the first published version of his autobiography at the request of Darwin's wife Emma, but it was restored in a later version by his grand-daughter, Nora Ballow.

Parallel to this development in the history of science, which weakened the position of the Church in the West politically, there was another development that supported the ascent of science as the ultimate authority on truth and, therefore, reality: its alliance with, and the successes of, technology. Technological developments, principally from the 19th century onwards, would make things possible that had hitherto been relegated to the realms of magic and mythology: to see an image of a person when she or he was not physically present (daguerreotype photography, 1839); to speak with others at a distance (telephone, 1871); and the ability to fly (1903), until then considered a most prohibitive realm, as the ancient Greek myth of Icarus suggested. Moreover, technology seemed to make the miracle possible, which was considered privileged territory of the Christian faith – although, in the famous Biblical story, it was Satan who tempted the Messiah to deliver a miracle (Matthew 4:1-11, Mark 1:12-13 and Luke 4:1-13) in exchange for unlimited power, which Jesus refused, ostensibly for not wanting to be followed because of his super-natural powers (according to Dostoyevsky, in the Great Inquisitor, the Church's desire for power and its association with the miracle constituted a deviation from the original spirit of Christianity, 1879-1880/1958, p. 319-320). Technology seemed to deliver the miracle directly and visibly, without a need for prayer or ritual. It did not require what in relation to religion would be called a 'leap of faith'.

In addition, technological progress helped produce advanced weaponry, making the connection between the attainment of truth, that is to say scientific-technological knowledge, and power, very tangible. Only one example of the consequences of this is the colonisation project, where it was, likely, mostly the superiority of weapons that made the conquest and exploitation of massive parts of other continents (notably the Americas and Africa) attainable for Europeans. And, especially in Latin America, invaded by Catholic Spain, the Church became one of the main political forces. In fact, it continues to be so to this day, even to the extent where it has recently 'delivered' its first Pope, Francesco. In addition to the darker pages of world history that are colonisation – which to this day have continued to leave a forceful signature on the state of affairs in international politics – it must be emphasised that technology gave new impetus to utopian dreaming, too. Albeit with a tone of regret, Martin Buber (1972, p. 18) argued that:

> … under the influence of a pan-technical current of thought, also utopia becomes an exclusively technical matter; the conscious human will, on which it traditionally rested, is now understood technically: like nature, society will now have to be controlled through technical calculations and technical constructions.

The idea that a technologisation of the environment can lead to a false consciousness has been elaborated by exponents of the Frankfurt School of social science, notably Herbert Marcuse. To Marcuse (1975, p. 172), the reconfiguration of nature through technology also entailed a reconfiguration of humanity. The view that developments in the fields of science and technology impact upon ethical conceptions, on ideas of what is good or not, is now quite broadly accepted. One need only think of the debate on abortion, for example. How, exactly, technology might have threatened the position of the Catholic Church becomes more clearly visible if the history of religion is approached via the central notion of control: as long as human beings feel they have no control over their destinies, they will be inclined to believe in an Almighty Power, which controls their fates. The reason for this is that there seems to be an inherent element in humanity that cannot believe in pure chance. Religion then functions as a sort of proxy, through which human beings can exert control over their life, and some form of agency – if not through direct action, then via worship of a deity that can intervene in nature or alternatively, is nature itself (Freud, 1927/1961, p. 19; on the use of magic see Malinowski, 1931, in Dobzhansky, 1969, p. 14).

As soon as human beings are able to understand (and predict) natural phenomena through scientific exploration and, simultaneously, to exert control over them by means of technological interventions, their feeling of autonomy will increase and they (or rather, we) will cease to feel the need for a proxy. Technology, in this view, is only the extension of ourselves, and we ourselves the source of knowledge of what is good and what not, which reflects, in essence, the main idea of humanism: the belief that holds that humanity itself is or at least should be the standard for its ethical rules and guidelines. To briefly return to the notion that, for now, we are referring mainly to European history, Dutch anthropologist Anil Ramdas, in the 1990s, associated a rationality based on science and technology explicitly with the Western world, in opposition to a holy, mystical, magical and irrational East (1993, p. 7). It is interesting to note that, over a 100 years earlier, Nietzsche had already said something quite similar, when asking (1872/1953, p. 141):

> Worauf weist das ungeheure historische Bedürfnis der unbefriedigten modernen Kultur, das Umsichsammeln zahlloser anderen Kulturen, das verzehrende Erkennenwollen, wenn nicht auf den Verlust des Mythus, auf den Verlust der mythischen Heimat, des mythischen Mutterschoßes?
>
> *What is indicated by the enormous historical need of unsatisfied modern culture, the act of surrounding itself with countless other cultures, the strong will to acknowledge, if not the loss of myth, then the loss of a mythical home, the mythical womb?*

It thus seems unsurprising that it is the 18th century movement of the Enlightenment that has often been considered constitutive of European identity. This age, preceded by the scientific revolution, is widely seen as that when humanity emancipated from superstition and through a greater understanding of nature became rational. Its essence is, at times, thought to have been summarised in Kant's expression *sapere aude*: dare to think (1784). In that sense, it was, in many places, a time of loss of power for the Church. Were they thinking the lines of the Ash'ari, when Horkheimer and Adorno argued, in 'Dialectics of enlightenment', that the Holocaust was a necessary consequence of the Enlightenment (1944/2007)? Or is it a coincidence when a society with certainly one of the most secular ethics of our time, the Netherlands, a place where gay marriage and euthanasia were first legally approved, was likened with dark pages of our history by the Church? (This not to say that this development was without critics: it has, for example, been critiqued by the Dutch-American sociologist James Kennedy, living in the Netherlands, who noted that the agenda to make taboos open to discussion already seems to imply a tacit consent (2002).)

A complication this revealed is that science itself – the scientific method – which had opened up the way to control over nature, does not seem to provide any criteria to evaluate issues ethically (except, possibly, via an ethic that says that what is allowed is limited only by what is possible). This has led to a remarkable paradox: while the power to act has grown exponentially through technological advances, the agreement on what that power should be used for, i.e. for what is considered good, has eroded along with old certainties due to progressing scientific enquiry.

The appearance of Islam

However, while, in Europe, secularisation has relatively strongly affected the position of the Christian religion and, in particular, that of the Catholic Church, its effects on Islam, including even on political Islam, seem more limited on the whole. Moreover, while it is often assumed that science and religion "have existed in more or less perpetual warfare" (Hedley Brooke, 2006, p. 293), at times, Islam has been viewed as an opponent rather than an ally in religion of Christianity: the supposed encounter between Islam and Christianity over the last 20 to 30 years was at times seen in a framework of a 'clash of civilisations', a term coined by Huntington (1993). The 2001 attack on the World

Trade Centre in New York City and the Pentagon in Washington, DC, has been presented as the apotheosis of this, even though these places were never important religious symbols. In understanding this, it is of importance to recall an important factor in the mind of most Western inhabitants of the early 21st century: they had celebrated the end of a bi-polar world order, wherein Western democracy was opposed to a communist world and, in particular, the Soviet Union. This perspective was well-captured by the North American thinker Francis Fukuyama, in his essay, which later became a book, 'The end of history' (the same trajectory as Huntington's 'Clash of civilisations?'). In this work, he described how and why a liberal-democratic social order defeated its main competing ideology (1992, p. 74-75) as illustrated by the collapse of the Soviet Union in 1991.

While there may have been earlier pre-shocks of a clash of civilisations between the Islamic and Western worlds, such as the Islamic revolution in Iran of 1978-1979, and the civil wars in Yugoslavia in the 1990s, the 2001 attacks and, in particular, their magnitude were still unexpected. In the view of many, Islam took up the role of a great 'Other'[18] that socialism had long held. Several conflicts were retrofitted into that perspective, including the Israel – Palestine conflict, the conflict in Sudan and even that in Chechnya. Certainly, that perception was subsequently reinforced by invasions of allied forces under the leadership of the United States of America in Afghanistan and Iraq. In Islamic rhetoric, these invasions were at times referred to as 'Crusades', emphasising a religious element in a wider conflict that it did not have in an increasingly secular West. In this regard, it is relevant to note that arguing that the inevitable outcome of history is liberal democracy, Fukuyama used Marx' weapon of historicism, which itself originated with Hegel, against him. This idea, that history has a pre-determined outcome, is one that socialism had in common with the narratives of the so-called 'religions of the book', the Abrahamic or monotheistic religions in gen-

---

[18] This is not to say that such an opposition has never existed before: the Ottoman occupations of parts of South-Eastern Europe and the Battles of Vienna, the Arab occupation of the Iberian peninsula (South-Western Europe) and the Crusades have also widely been perceived as confrontations between Islam and Christianity.

eral: in Christianity, the end of history consists of the foundation of a New Jerusalem; in Islam, an ultimate victory would lead to the re-establishment of the original Islamic State, or 'Umma, worldwide; for several branches of Judaism, this is Israel.

These anticipated 'ends of history' are, in fact, utopias: ideal social orders. Lewis Mumford (1922/1959, p. 59-60) distinguished between utopias of reconstruction and utopias of escape. The difference between these types of utopias is that a utopia of reconstruction can or should be brought about by human action, while a utopia of escape is realised without human intervention. The religious utopias would be classified as utopias of escape, as they are contingent upon divine action (although in Islam and Judaism this is often realised through human beings, being 'instruments of God'). The utopia described in Plato's Republic, by contrast, is a utopia of reconstruction, because it delivers an exact programme, with rules, of how to realise this ideal society. So is Communist society.

One specific problem with such utopias – including Marx' – was, and is, that if the end of history is known, everything that stands between it and the present moment can and probably should be eliminated. It was for reasons such as these that Popper, this time as a political philosopher, severely criticised historicism, the conception that history has a predetermined course and outcome. For example, in one interview (1994, p. 8) he said that there is no necessary and inevitable outcome of history, but that the course of history is determined by individual decisions of individual persons. Until this day, Popper's statement is highly relevant. In addressing the integration of migrants in European societies, for example, reference is often made to a 'sociological' kind of thinking, i.e. thinking in structures rather than actions. Time, it is said, will assimilate newcomers into European societies. But time is not an autonomous agent – it is human actions within time, not time itself, that shape the course of history (e.g. Bilagher 2007, p. 32).

Certainly, utopias, at least as a literary genre (Manuel & Manuel, 1982) have historically often been perceived as social commentary: as covert criticism of the rules of the time. More's Utopia (published in 1515), for example, was meant to emphasise the discrepancy between what a state could or even should look like and the rule of King Henry VII in the England at the time (Labrie 1989, p. 208). Something similar can be said of the Solar State (or 'City of the Sun'), which was written by Tommaso Campanella in 1602. Campanella, incidentally, wrote a defence of Galileo when the latter was trialled for his scientific ideas (see above). Some have said that, in comparison with other religions, and specifically Christianity, one characteristic of Islam is that it does not see itself as one way among other, different, but potentially equivalent ways to metaphysical and cosmological truth, but claims to reflect a unique, ultimate truth. Its utopia would for that reason be incompatible with pluralism. It suggests that the Qur'an is understood to be the final message of a Divine Creator to mankind, which superseded the previous Books (the Torah and the Christian Bible, or 'Injil'). These previous books are said to convey the same messages as Islam, in principle, and so these books are incorporated into Islam; but they are also thought to have been delivered in an imperfect way.

Some of these ideas seem indeed to be encoded in the Qur'an itself. For example, Sura Ali Imraan (3) says that Islam is the true religion (Aya 20), and that other religions than Islam are not allowed (Aya 86); Sura An Nisa (4), Aya 48, says that Islam is the right religion, thereby implying that the other religions are not right religions. The edition of the Ahmadiyya movement contains a foreword not merely explaining why Islam is the right religion, but also explaining why other religions – not only those 'of the Book' - are erroneous. Still, it is a highly problematic claim that Islam is alone in its suggestions of its own uniqueness; not only because it is not factual, but because great religions have so many faces. Islam alone, for example, is sub-divided in the Sunni group, who believe in a spiritual succession of the Prophet Mohammad; and the Shi'a group, who believe in the physical succession of Mohammad. There are also sub-divisions within these groups: for example, the Alevites among the Shi'a, and the Druze, who are not considered real Muslims by many other Muslims, in general.

It is also problematic because it seeks a certain exceptionalism for Islam as a religion that has a difficult relation with peace while, rather, the general claim that religions seek peace seems rather naïve. While the Catholic Church may have had the Second Vatican Council, it has also had the Inquisition, the colonisation of Latin America in which the Catholic Church was highly complicit and Christianity's Messiah Jesus has said that he had come to "bring the sword" (Matthew 10:34). This is not to mention the Christian thought portrayed in Dante's Divine Comedy. Dante's comedy describes his travel through the afterlife, that is, inferno, purgatory and paradise (1320/2008). According to Dante Alighieri, even the Prophets of the Old Testament have to dwell in inferno, albeit in the outer circles, where punishment is less severe, because of the simple fact that they were born before the age of mercy, which started with the coming of the Messiah.

In Hinduism, the Deity Krishna incited the warrior Arjuna to fight against a related clan. In fact, he argued that, for a person of the kṣatria (warrior) class, it would be a sin not to fight (Verse 2:31 of the Bhagavad Gita), of course as long as it is for a good cause or, rather, the purpose of one's existence (it is striking that, for Plato, in the Republic, injustice was not to act in accordance with the purpose of one's existence, suggesting an early influence). Similarly, in the Jewish Bible, called the Torah, we see that God ordered Moses to enter into the land of Canaan – roughly present-day Israel and the Occupied Palestinian Territories – and to kill every Canaanite: man, woman and child (Deuteronomy 20:16-18). Naturally, this is considered to be for a good cause as well, that is to say, the future of the Jewish people.

In principle, probably few would argue with the legitimacy of a fight for a good cause in general. In line with this, Saint Augustine (Augustinus, 426/2007), born in the 4th century CE and widely understood to have been Christianity's first major philosopher, is credited with the invention of the concept of a righteous war (p. 952 – although Livy referred to this as well, see Machiavelli, 1532/1998, p. 158) when arguing that "every human being strives for peace through war, and not for war through peace" (Augustinus, 426/2007, p. 957). In Islam, while not formally one of its five pillars, warfare is present in the form of the small Jihad or Holy War and the Qur'an, Islam's main sacred text, contains several indications for how a righteous war should be fought (see, for example, Sura Ali Imran (3), Aya 14). The problem here is, naturally, to determine what really is a just cause – or what is a rightful utopia. For example, there likely are many people of Jewish identity who may believe that Israel is a rightful utopia and who conclude from this that a war against Christian and Muslim Palestinians is therefore just, as a means, to attain utopia.

For some Muslims, the fight of non-state violent organisations could be perceived as a justified one because of the United States-led invasions, for example, in Afghanistan and Iraq. Such a perception may be strengthened by a view of Western secularisation as a sign of decadence, and even amorality, where Muslims remain 'guardians of virtue', which they defend against and sometimes in a West that manifests itself as a value-less society. According to Dutch-American writer Leon de Winter, in an article in the New York Times (16 July 2005), this occurred in the Netherlands, in part due to the fact that Christian Calvinist values, which still form the substructure of Netherlands society, are in operation under the surface, and therefore not recognised by (some) immigrants. Be that as it may, Nietzsche saw something positive in religious war in general, as he said in his 'Gay science' (1882/1973: Third Book, Par. 144, p. 169):

> Der Grösste Fortschritt der Massen war bis jetzt der Religionskrieg: denn er beweist, dass die Masse angefangen hat, Begriffe mit Ehrfurcht zu behandeln.
>
> *The greatest progress of the masses has so far been the holy war: because it proves that the masses have begun to treat concepts with respect.*

The French philosopher René Descartes would probably completely disagree with Nietzsche on this point. In the year 1637, he published his 'Discourse on Method', in which he presented a philosophy based on mathematical principles. This was built on his initial thesis *cogito ergo sum*, usually translated as 'I think, therefore I am', which he considered to be beyond doubt. Stephen Toulmin, in 'Cosmopolis', interpreted Descartes' attempt to renew philosophy as a reaction to the terror of the Thirty Years War (1618 to 1648),[19] a war between Catholics and Protestants in the heart of Europe, and notorious for its cruelty. It left entire areas depopulated. To prevent similar wars in the future, Descartes attempted to find a common principle that could be equally valid for all human beings, regardless of their religion, and form a starting point for shared discussions on values (and therefore not an end point of history, as represented by a utopia). According to Descartes, any human knowledge could potentially be based on deception – except for the fact of awareness itself, which he considered self-evident. This, according to Descartes, was a basic idea that all people could share and on which further shared understandings could be founded. This idea, according to Toulmin, is at the basis of what he called the 'hidden agenda of modernity' (1990, p. 56). Toulmin saw a 'quest for certainty' in this because, if "Europeans were to avoid falling into a sceptical morass, they had, it seemed, to find *something* to be 'certain' about" (id., p. 55).

The incentives to undertake a similar enterprise, to devise a new framework for common understandings across religious and paradigmatic divides in this time of social, religious and cultural division, possibly brought about in no small part by globalisation, seem overwhelming. We can take the encounter between Islam and Christianity to reflect a pattern similar to that other encounter between east and west (socialism vs. liberal democracy) or between emerging countries China and India and established economies (such as the G7). If the world as a whole is facing severe challenges, such as the maintenance of biodiversity and climate change, then how can we approach these from a foundation of shared human values?

What would be needed to devise such a framework is a rational foundation from which to identify the merits, first of religion in general and, subsequently, of manifestations of religion such as Islam, Christianity,

---

[19] According to Popper (1963/2006, p. 446), "[e]veryone learned from Marx that the development even of ideas cannot be fully understood if the history of ideas is treated … without mentioning the conditions of their origin and the situation of their originators".

Judaism and Hinduism specifically, in order to distinguish them from misconceptions; to purify, therefore, the influential religions from misinterpretations and superstitions. In pursuing this mission, I agree with Horkheimer and Adorno (1944/2007) when they suggested that "religious fanaticism is the sign of its falsehood" (p. 33). This should not be understood, however, as a project to develop a new utopia or even as a search for a common denominator or synthesis of existing utopias. Rather than in the end of time, I am interested in its beginning or origin. My thesis is that an open society and religions are not incompatible with one another – what is required is to give the Emperor *only* what is hers (or his), and not more than that.

To begin giving an indication of what this means, it is necessary to observe that, because a religion normally represents a comprehensive belief system, naturally reflecting and penetrating several or even all domains of life – the ethical, political, philosophical – it can be adhered to on several levels: first, and most frequently, a religion is adhered to on the level of simple obedience to the regulations stipulated by it. This is not necessarily wrong. For example, if a rule in Christianity says that one should not kill anyone, and this corresponds to a valuable ethical rule of whichever origin, then obedience, rather than deep understanding, is sufficient to do what is good or rather: not evil. This level of faith is said to have been the most important for Ukrainian Hasidic leader Nahman of Bratslav, for example, according to Cohn-Sherbook (2007, p. 155) and, for this reason, Nahman of Bratslav is said to have been critical of the study of philosophy. According to Cohen (1921/2021), however, historically there were four Jewish exegetic methods: that of 'peshat' (simple), literal interpretation; 'remez' (allusion), allegorical interpretation; 'darash' (exposition), homiletical (sermonic) comment; and 'sod' (mystery), i.e. esoteric teaching (p. 24).

On another level, therefore, it is possible to adhere to a religion in terms of understanding. The difference is that, whereas obedience of a rule entails accepting it without questioning or discussion, understanding means knowing why that rule exists. The rule that it is not allowed to steal may exist because if there were not such a rule, it would be difficult for people to own property, which in turn would not encourage anyone to work hard to gain wealth. If everyone would act as if such a moral rule did not exist, progress of society as a whole would be inhibited; this would in turn inflict negatively on the well-being of the individual members, including the transgressors of the rule. The rule of praying five times a day, in Islam (one of the five pillars of that religion), may have the function of bringing believers to contemplate, bring them in touch with an eternal reality, similar to Plato's ideal world. In this way, religion tends to pervade all aspects of life for Muslims. Indeed, in most Muslim countries, religion is omnipresent (civil marriages, for example, are prohibited in several Arab countries) but metaphorical interpretations may not be common. Surely, the emergence of scholars such as Nasr Abu Zayd in Egypt pointed towards a possible renaissance of Muslim hermeneutics, but his excommunication from Islam in 1995 suggests that his ideas may not be part of mainstream. This may well be because the Qur'an is generally taken to be the literal and undiluted Word of God, delivered to man, the Prophet Muhammad, via the angel Gabriel (*Jibril* or جبريل).

The importance of this 'second level' of understanding religion may be amplified by the global context in which we increasingly live, one that has been described as a 'global village': one where people of different religions, ethnicities and cultures or civilisations, as Huntington would say, live together in often urban spaces in- and outside of their traditional territories; often, in open societies. While this global encounter, which is taking place between and within nations,[20] on the one hand offers great potential for cultural and economic enrichment, it also entails a real, but underestimated, risk of intercultural misunderstanding and conflict. Religion is, mainly for the reason mentioned above, i.e. that it is complex to determine what a rightful utopia is, one of the potential sources of such conflicts; even within nations of people with predominantly a similar ethnic background (e.g. India, Iraq and Lebanon), religion can create different points of view that result in violent

---

[20] The 'formal' starting point of this encounter can probably be dated to the foundation of the United Nations, in 1945 (and its predecessor the League of Nations, founded in 1920), as the first truly global intergovernmental organisation.

conflict.[21] It is, therefore, time for a broad, rather than specific, philosophy to further contribute to this discussion.

I believe that the main obstacle for inter-religious understanding, which is also the main contention atheists raised against proponents of religion in general, lies, roughly, in the tension between reason and revelation. It is not extraordinary to separate religion from philosophy via arguments that say that philosophy is rational, and appealing to the rational dimension of humanity, where religion appeals to more than only this. That is to say, it appeals to the 'whole of the human being', which includes our feelings, intuitions and spirituality (cf. Cohn-Sherbok on Abraham Geiger 2007, p. 73). This view I do not contest. What I do contest is the view that because religion spans a wider spectrum than philosophy, elements of it are inaccessible to reason and therefore have to be subject to dogma. This does of course not preclude the first level of religious life; after all, not every believer needs to be a theologian. But it does mean that some sort of ecumenical discussion on the second level is necessary to manage globalisation.

So this defines the mission before us. Nevertheless, before embarking on the quest to demonstrate the rationality of religion so as to be able to separate it from superstition, dogma and religious politics (which are not always the same), we have to briefly turn to the main idea behind the notion that there cannot or should not be such a rationality (I will address this question in greater detail later). The argument is that, to the contrary of the 'mind of God', the human mind is fallible and, as what we call reason is inherently human reason, its achievements cannot be compared with the fruits of Divine Reason. Therefore, to find truth, the human being is inherently dependent on revelation. Clearly, in relation to the mentioned levels of adherence to religious tenets, this

---

[21] This is, of course, a simplification: genetic analyses do reveal different origins of, for example, Christian and Muslim Lebanese. This can to some extent be explained by taboos on inter-religious marriages there and the fact that Christians in Lebanon may have descended mainly from the original Syriac, rather than Phoenician, population of Greater Syria. The Muslims at least in part descend from the Muslim invaders from the Sa'udi peninsula. In Northern Ireland, similarly, the Protestant population is broadly understood to be of Scottish heritage, while the Catholics are considered originally Irish.

view mainly supports the experience of religion on the first level, of obedience, with greater emphasis than on the second one, of understanding.

There are obviously some problems with this rationale, of which the main one seems to be the unreasoned opposition between human reason and Divine Reason. It seems difficult to accept without further argumentation that human reason and Divine Reason should be fundamentally different types of reason, rather than that the latter is the perfection and completion of the former. Accepting the possibility that it is possible for human beings to have access to Divine reason, the first thing to do is establish a foundation for religion: a rational basis from which the main tenets of faiths may be understood, rather than only obeyed. And here, philosophy can come to the aid of theology.

The philosophical objections against religion and their refutation: New atheism

In what we usually refer to as the West,[22] and probably mainly in North-Western Europe, the irrationality of faith has relatively recently been emphasised in the public discourse. This has probably been done most forcefully by a movement called 'New Atheism' and, in particular, the 'Four Horsemen of Atheism' Richard Dawkins, Daniel Dennett, Sam Harris and the late Christopher Hitchens. Among these, the most well-known in Europe might be the biologist Richard Dawkins, whose book 'The God Delusion' (2007) has at the time engendered a lively, public debate and, obviously, dissident opinions.[23] Its essential thesis is that religion is inherently dangerous because it is delusional and almost certainly refers to a reality that does not exist. It may not be a coincidence that two of the 'Horsemen' and their ideas originate from

---

[22] With West, here I refer mainly to the countries of Western Europe and North America, although I realise this term may not denote a real cultural continuum. I use this roughly in the sense of a civilisation as per Huntington, in the realisation that cultural spaces are and will continue to be shifting.

[23] One of them called simply 'The Dawkins delusion?' by Alister McGrath and his wife Joanna Collicutt McGrath (2007).

a country whose main ecclesiastical entity is the Church of England. This has been referred to as the most pragmatic of churches, based in a country where atheism is popular, in line with the empiricism that the anthropologist Kate Fox (author of 'Watching the English', 2004, p. 206; see also p. 354) perceived as inherent in the British national character. Interestingly, Stein (2009, p. 216) argued that:

> For fear of 'falling into the hands of the living God', sinners take refuge in theoretical denial, but their flight only leads to another kind of dread [*Angst*]: dread of the naught [*Nichts*].

The representation of biologists – scientists of nature – among 'active atheists' (among the 'Horsemen' Harris, in addition to Dawkins) and the strong position of this discipline in the United Kingdom is possibly not surprising either given that Britain was the home of Charles Darwin. The same Darwin whose theory of evolution, mentioned earlier, has been perceived as final blow to a Church whose claim to truth had not differentiated between scientific and religious truth (a distinction Dawkins himself contested, 2007, pp. 79-80). Could this have anything to do with the fact that biology seems closer to the physical and physics closer to the metaphysical? In saying this, one is not only reminded of Aristotle who said that between biology (where evolution theory comes from) and physics, the latter is the more fundamental science, but also of Wegter-McNelly, who mentioned the "eagerness with which many in modern cultures look to physicists for answers to … ultimate life-questions" (2006, p. 156). Dobzhansky (1969), on the other hand, surmised that biology might well be more relevant to philosophy as it is "of general humanistic interest and import" (p. 2).

The idea that God and living nature, the subject of biology, are one and the same, or two sides of the same coin, has been attributed to Spinoza in his main work 'Ethics' (*'Deus sive natura'*, 1677/1981). However, the idea can be found earlier with the Italian monk Tommaso Campanella. Manuel and Manuel (1982, p. 266) note that Campanella declared, according to 'terror-struck witnesses': "There is no God. There is only nature which we call God." This view conveys, among other things, the idea that humanity stands in a relation to its Creator as it stands to nature – a nature it originates in but is nonetheless distinct from. This suggests that humanity, in the greater scheme of things, understands itself as existing vis-à-vis nature, which it considers an inescapable force that it encounters not only in its surroundings (the land houses are built on, the earth we take our food from, the sea we navigate on) but also in itself (i.e. in its instincts), with which it is therefore forced to a sometimes uneasy cohabitation.

The Dutch historian and philosopher of science Chunglin Kwa identified two ways for humanity of dealing with this situation: either nature, through a symbolic conversion to a God or gods, could be pacified and conformed to (Judaism, Hinduism), in line with the principle 'if you can't beat it, join it'; or it had to be outwitted, which was the solution of the ancient Greeks (1991, p. 6). The ancient Greeks had many gods, constituting their pantheon (Πάνθεον) who, Kwa observed, were strikingly similar in their nature to human beings, including an inclination towards typically human flaws. The Greek gods could even procreate with mortal human beings, producing demigods,[24] in a way similar to Hinduism. Therefore, if human beings were smart enough, they could outwit the gods. As it is not difficult to associate natural phenomena with the Greek gods[25] (Zeus[26] with lightning, Poseidon with the sea, and so on) this suggested that, if human beings were sufficiently clever, they could control nature via technology.

This could also go wrong and, if it did, the perpetrators were severely punished. Probably the most well-known example of this is Prometheus, who tried to steal fire from the gods. It is not a coincidence that Prometheus' torch is incorporated in the emblem of the Netherlands' oldest technical university at Delft. This general cosmogonic outlook of the

---

[24] Which would technically speaking make them part of the same species, as it is a biological given that only members of one same species – or race - can procreate (see Edward O. Wilson, 2003, p. 217 in Kroonenberg, 2007, p. 289).

[25] And, incidentally, not only with the Greek gods: some Norse Gods, such as Thor (Thuner in the Anglo-Saxon pantheon), were also associated with natural phenomena. Thor was the god of thunder.

[26] The Hindu deity Indra seems quite reminiscent of the figure of Zeus.

Greeks, Kwa said, at least in part explains why a certain type of science and technology originated in Europe. This would be more complex in a monotheistic setting. Even though it might be facile to identify Greek religion or Hinduism with polytheism *tout court* (Hinduism has uniting concepts emphasising Oneness of all, on an abstract level, such as the structural principle of the universe, *atmān*), it is true that, for Judaism, human existence is founded on an agreement or covenant between the Creator and the Jewish people. Whenever this is broken, and the Jews do not listen to their Prophets – for example, Jeremiah – they are punished: this is the course of their history as recorded in the Old Testament or Torah (הָרוֹת). This suggests more difficult conditions for the development of science and technology.

The main ideas presented earlier, that increased control of nature, via the proxies of science and technology, established humanity as firmly separate from nature, and the one that God and nature are two sides of the same coin may, to an extent, help explain the rise of secularism in the Western world. The weakened position of religion in Europe runs, to an extent, parallel to a perceived decrease in the power of the forces of nature to control human lives. Through technological progress, this nature has become so weak that it needs an 'ecological movement' to protect it, rather than that there is a perceived need to protect humanity from nature (or at least a need to regulate this relation, between nature / gods and human beings, the historical function of religion) – in other words, the helplessness versus nature, which, in Freud's view constitutes the origin of religion (1927/1961, p. 19), did not exist anymore. Theoretically, at least, this may change with the importance of climate change rising on the public agenda.

So then, what is wrong with this, if anything? The problem here is that the basic argument that religion refers to a reality that simply does not exist, is incorrect. Religion does refer to an existing reality. While I will explain this further in the sections to come, it is first important to see that those who defend a more or less pure atheism do so by indicating that there exists no empirical evidence for the arguments that most religions have in common and, most of all, for the existence of a God,

Deity or superior Being. It is important, at this point, to separate such a hypothesis from specific religious beliefs. For example, it is possible that a Deity exists but that a particular religion is incorrect in making a specific statement of what this Deity wants or expects from us. Several religions, for example, suggest that men are of greater importance than women, in that men can be spiritual leaders, while women cannot. This can be perfectly flawed, without having as a necessary consequence that religion as a whole refers to a realm that does not exist.

The fundamental oversight of many atheists, I believe, is that they do not see that religion refers, by definition, to a transcendental realm and there does not, necessarily, exist any empirical evidence for it. This seems underpinned by a preference for a specific philosophical orientation in the dialogue between idealism (spiritualism) and materialism (physicalism), or more generally, the dichotomy between universals and particulars, which, according to Rorty, constituted the main problem of the last 2,500 years of Western philosophy. It might not be a coincidence that idealism is traditionally associated with Continental philosophy, while materialism is rather perceived as part of an Anglo-American tradition (see Popper, 1963/2006, p. 4)[27] and the 'four Horsemen' hail from Great Britain and the United States. The ideological position of the Horsemen, and many if not all atheists, which they do not always seem to perceive of as an ideological position and rather often seem to take for granted, is that matter (in a broad sense) is the foundation of all reality. This, of course, aligns very well with Popper's principle of demarcation (1963/2006), but one should remember that Popper devised this not to separate truth from falsehood, or real from unreal, but science from pseudo-science. And, of course, Popper saw that another criterion might be needed to evaluate metaphysical hypotheses. Philosophically, thus, these atheists choose materialism over idealism – a choice that can itself not be justified empirically.

To be clear on terminology, here, with materialism, I refer to the assump-

---

[27] Surely, this is a generalisation as, for example, the German philosopher Schopenhauer said, in his main work 'The World as Will and Representation', that none prevails over the other (1818/1996, p. 71).

tion that, in essence, mind is a product of matter while, according to idealism, the opposite is true, i.e. matter is, in essence, a product of mind. In response to the extreme materialistic claim that anything intangible is not real, the Swiss psychoanalyst Carl Jung responded that, since all sensory perception is always transferred through the mind, it may as well be said that the mind is the source of all reality (1982, p. 16):

> It is a preposterous prejudice that existence could only be physical. We could just as well posit the opposite, that physical existence is our own [subjective] conclusion, because we only know anything at all about matter in as far as we have access to mental images, which are transferred to us by our senses.

No materialist has been able to convincingly refute this argument and, strictly speaking, this is not possible, as Schopenhauer conceded (he referred to this as 'theoretical egoism', 1818/1996, I, p. 163). Regarding the existence of others, Stein argued that "*for me* their existence does not have this absolute factualness; rather, it can just as much be doubted as the existence of material things" (2009, p. 375). Interestingly, this extreme idealist position leads to a similar outcome as the extreme materialist one held by the Austrian thinker Ernst Mach. Mach argued that: "Not bodies produce sensations, but element-complexes (sensation-complexes) constitute the bodies. When the physicist considers the bodies as the permanent reality, the 'elements' as the transient appearance, he does not realise that all 'bodies' are only mental symbols for element-complexes (sensation-complexes)" (1922/1987, p. 23). While these are extreme positions, it is quite evident that what we commonly refer to as the intangible and tangible, intersect with one another. With the word objects, we describe entities in the physical world; with the word concepts, metaphysical or non-material entities. The materialist basic rationale is, often, that objects are real because they are tangible. However, and while this does not affect the tangibility of an object, one could argue that the perception of an object could not exist without the existence of a related concept in the mind of the perceiver.

An important example from Plato's work may help clarify this: there are many objects in the natural world that can be classified as chairs. However, none of these are exactly the same. So, even though the chairs in the world are distinct objects, they can still be attributed to this one category of chairs. Without the existence of such a category (or concept) of things, the object itself could possibly be discerned as an object in general, but not specifically as a chair. Therefore, the object of the chair is created by its concept and, in this sense, conceptual reality creates tangible reality. This is mirrored in an interesting way in the famous Biblical verse from John (1:1), which says that, in the Beginning, there was the Word (i.e. the concept). An oft-referred to explanation of this aspect of Plato's ontology is the one offered by Bertrand Russell in his history of western philosophy. In this work, he suggested that as all particular cats can be recognised as cats, according to his explanation of Plato's theory, they must all have some sort of 'cattiness' (1945/2007, p. 123). In my view, this suggests the existence of an empirical substance, which I find difficult to recognise in Plato's theory. As a consequence, it might lead to an incorrect impression of Plato's thought.

This principle that metaphysical entities, i.e. concepts, bring about physical entities or objects is true also in a broader sense: a country, such as, say, The Netherlands, cannot be discerned in physical reality because it is a concept without a related object.[28] There is the territory, but this is not the country itself; there is the Head of State, but neither is she or he the country; there is a people that are called the Dutch, but even this is not this country. The country is only a concept, which is nonetheless real in the minds of many people. As such, it creates other concepts such as citizenship and, as a derivative of this, illegal immigrants; but it also creates concrete objects, such as the Parliament buildings or an infrastructure developed through a national mobilisation of resources and expertise. In this example, intangible ideas intervene in empirical reality. To an extent, they create it.[29] What is necessary to realise here is that the natural sciences are the sciences of human perception, the reign of the empirical or, in the words of Schopenhauer, the domain

---

[28] In this sense, this example is similar to that of the university presented earlier.
[29] I used a similar example in an article in the magazine Gamma (2006, pp. 42–44).

of reality which is regulated by the '*Satz vom Grunde*' (1818/1996, pp. 34-44). According to this principle, every manifestation must be caused by something.

The natural sciences examine the manifestations of perception, but not perception itself. The main instruments underpinning these sciences are concepts, such as measurement, taxonomy, association, classification, hierarchy, hypothesis, point, conclusion, inference and so on, which have all in common that they cannot be found in nature. Even Einstein has, as Ilse Rosenthal-Schneider expressed it (1980, p. 88), emphasised several times that "it is wrong to assume that we can arrive at any concepts by deriving them from sense experience … *only*." To understand where concepts come from, we have to understand something about ourselves and, as Dobzhansky (1969) said, to "'know thyself', scientific knowledge is palpably insufficient" (p. 9). In this regard, philosophy can come to our aid. Kant, in particular, observed that perception itself is a combination of sensory impressions and concepts or ideas from a Platonic, metaphysical (or: beyond physical) reality, which is described by Kant's a priori categories – time, space and causality. The notions of *a priori* and *a posteriori* knowledge in Kant's philosophy denote, and differentiate between, roughly, the form and the content of human experience (1781/1990, p. 2). For example, we see a chair (content) at a certain place and time (form).

Kant's unique contribution to philosophy, at times referred to as a 'Copernican revolution', is that with him, experience was not anymore understood to be something external that is imposed upon one and perceived through a set of senses. It is meaning, originally condensed, unfolding itself through the ordering principles of the mind, such as time (a priori knowledge). In this way, meaning, which is by itself unitary and undivided, can unfold itself through events, which exist as such for sensory experience. The human faculty of *Vernunft* (reason) may, subsequently, recognise that original meaning in the patterns of the perceived events. This can be illustrated by means of a simple thought experiment: if experiences were completely at random, i.e. took place or were experienced in a random temporal order, and if, as a consequence, there were no coherence between them (as what would establish the coherence would normally be a temporal sequence), experience as such would not be possible. The result would be complete confusion, which would not only result in not understanding the sequence of perceptions that one would be presented with but, in fact, an absence of perception itself. In other words, for perception or consciousness to exist, there must be a structure to the experiences forming that perception. This structure is normally chronological, or, rather, the structure is chronology itself. Chronology makes the ordering principles of the mind, such as causality, possible.

The idea that cause and effect exist, that something can lead to something else or, alternatively stated, that one reality can induce another, is at the root of the experience of subjectivity. If a human being would not have the notion that something he or she does will or could potentially change reality, then the subject might not think that it exists – in as far as existence is not only related to mere perceptions of reality,[30] but also the ability to act in and on it (incidentally, for Schopenhauer, this was sufficient to reject the proposition of extreme idealism). This is the mentioned Copernican revolution: Kant did not only identify the basic structures, or prerequisites, of consciousness – he also redefined the relation between these structures and their content (i.e. the perception of objects). Whereas the tacit assumption in philosophy had until Kant been that perception created the structures of consciousness (say, the occurrence of events creates time), Kant turned this notion around. He asserted that space and time are rather than a framework within which events may occur, ordering agents, helping human consciousness grasp meaning by dissecting it into specific events, occurring in a chronological, meaningful order. We are therefore not atomic robots strolling through a landscape that we perceive or not but, rather, our experience is itself essence or meaning, dissected into portions that are fed to us in and through time.

---

[30] I recognise that Descartes based the supposition of existence on perception alone, even though most translations translate 'cogito ergo sum' as 'I think' or even 'I am thinking, therefore I exist' (1637/2008).

This Kantian revolution implies the existence of something eternal that exists out of time, while our experience is equal to time. As such, this other 'thing' is alien to our direct experience, which is contingent upon time as, as we have discussed, experience cannot exist outside of the here and now. In this view, once again, the metaphysical creates the physical, or rather the experience of the physical, which is all the physical really is, as Mach wrote (see earlier reference);[31] only, the emphasis has subtly shifted because that abstract entity creating reality is meaning. Indeed, Kant, in the 'Critique of Pure Reason', already wrote that thinking about time, thought thinks of itself (1781/1956, pp. 76-77). Time is, it seems, in fact, fair to say, consciousness itself or, as Horkheimer and Adorno expressed this, the inner organisational form of individuality (1944/2007, p. 62). Stein (2009, p. 339) formulated this idea slightly differently when saying that: "Just as corporeal matter fills … space with its qualities, so the life of the soul fills time with its qualities".

---

[31] In 'Conjectures and Refutations', Popper noted the similarity of some of Mach's themes and ideas with themes and ideas developed by Berkeley. He summarised one of Berkeley's notions (in De Motu) as follows: "physical bodies are nothing but their qualities. Their appearance is their reality" (1963/2006, p. 227; second sentence emphasised in the original).

3

The theory of two times: Truth and the structure of the mind

The architecture of perception

So far, I argued that in what can broadly be called the Western world, religion has been perceived as under attack. This is, firstly, due to a challenge from the natural sciences and, secondly, because of a confrontation – encounter – between religions. In particular, I referred to the 'new atheist' objections against religion. I then pointed out that (a) there is a difference between manifestations of specific religions and religious reality in general and, concomitantly, objections against these; and (b) that the natural sciences are sciences of the perceptions of the mind, not of the mind itself. If perceptions, empirical or not, are thought to hold the key to reality, then an examination of the source of these perceptions, i.e. the mind, seems to be in order. And, in this pursuit, philosophy can guide us.

When we say that perception is inevitably in time, we are making an observation on a meta-level: we are capable of saying something about the mind, and about experience, that is itself not rooted in experience. We are able to say something about the nature of experience, rather than relate an experience. The mere possibility of this implies that the mind, and the process of thinking, is not only occurring in consciousness. This was probably the most important discovery of the psychoanalytic movement. Freud, its founder, and other exponents of this tradition recognised that the mind is not only working in the here and now, upon which consciousness depends, but that there is also a memory, a past and a sub- or unconscious part of the mind that functions as the 'embodiment' of that past in the mind. According to Freud, "[t]he great majority of philosophers call only that psychological [*psychisch*] which is a phenomenon of consciousness [i.e. a perception, MB]. The conscious world, for them, coincides with the extent of the psyche" (1924/1991, p. 97). With these philosophers, he very probably did not mean Arthur Schopenhauer (1818/1996, II, p. 175) who, already in 1818, had observed that consciousness "is only the surface of our minds, of which, like of the earth, we do not know the interior but only the [outer] shell."

To some extent, of course, this is understandable if we think of the mind as existing only in the here and now, in a sort of eternal cycle, where every moment seems eternally new, and where, therefore, no accumulation of experiences and thus growth could occur. Again, there would be experience, but it would probably not have much meaning, as the mind cannot develop any sense of context. The judgement whether a morning is beautiful or not can hardly be made without the memory of at least some previous mornings, against which the relative beauty of the morning that is the subject of experience can be evaluated. Therefore, if a certain event has taken place in the past of a person, this would not be part of the content of the direct experience anymore but, given sufficient impression, it could still colour a person's present experience. This has to do with what the Swiss psychoanalyst Jung, initially a student of Freud's, called personal unconsciousness, which for Freud was simply unconsciousness. If a person would once have had a bad experience with a dog, say, and would have forgotten that, but would encounter another dog in the here and now – in present experience - then she or he might still be afraid of this animal due to the previous experience.

Although, naturally, memory is there for people to learn, in some situations, and those that were of interest to the psychoanalysts, certainly Freud, memories could become an impediment to normal functioning. This was the case if there was some type of dysfunction at work, which could develop into a pathology where the mechanisms of the unconsciousness were not sufficiently clear to the person in question, or the original experience was forgotten, whereby one's reactions would seem inexplicable to oneself. In such a situation a person would develop counter-reactions of which the nature were unclear to him- or herself and thus, a neurosis would ensue (1925/1991, p. 40). The psychoanalyst would then try to help the person by re-establishing a link between conscious experience and unconsciousness. One interesting example of this is Freud's case study of the 'rat man' (1909/1989). This man, a client of Freud's, told him how a befriended, wealthy couple would occasionally let their daughter stay at his estate for the weekend. On such occasions, the slightly older man would seek some quasi-sexual benefits from the girl. In his interactions with the man, Freud noticed that he would always pay him not only with clean, but also ironed bills. The man would justify this with a remark of the type that 'one never knows through which kind of filthy hands such bills go'. Of course, objectively, the rat man's hands were filthy. Freud interpreted this overreaction in one area (his payment with cleaned bills) as compensation for his filthiness in another (his treatment of the girl). However, this mechanism was invisible to the consciousness of the man, i.e. unconscious. To Freud, healing a patient meant making this unconscious content visible, that is to say, conscious.

Memory can be part of an individual, but also of a collective. For example, Toulmin and Goodfield narrated how Josephus of Alexandria said that the Greeks, in contrast to the ancient Jews, had no history, and how, after a number of generations, they were "plunged into a realm of legend" (1982, p. 28). The implication of this is that having no history resulted in a cyclical fashion of life, without real progress, because having no access to lessons learnt of the past, one would continue to reinvent the wheel. Or, worse, one would feel that the course of humanity is not leading anywhere, except to the place it started from – a realisation which certainly resembles the way one approaches realities in the here and now. Naturally, this view can be criticised, not just because the ancient Greeks had several historians, such as Thucydides, but also because it excludes the possibility that mythologies can contain similar lessons as formal history, albeit in a metaphorical or allegoric veil, as Campbell, for example, argued in 'The Power of Myth' (1988, pp. 15 and 22). It is, widely understood that narratives such as stories for children are often intended to convey moral notions[32] and the story of

---

[32] Whether good or bad: some children stories are criticised because they convey a 'hidden' ethic that is not considered pedagogically sound anymore. Several authors, for example, noted that the story of Thomas the Tank Engine contains moral signals that condemn non-conformism.

Prometheus also contains an implicit warning.[33] It seems rather likely that the registers of ancestral lineage in the Old Testament, or Torah, fade from possibly (partly) real registers into mythology. A question we may have to pose ourselves is: which contain more real information, the birth registers or the myths?

Jung, before Campbell, also recognised the truth in myth: in his further development of Freud's theory, he identified not only the personal unconsciousness, like Freud, but also a collective unconsciousness (even though Schopenhauer seems to have been very close to discovering this, see 1818/1996, II, p. 422). Rather than a collective memory written in books, or orally delivered through generations of civilisations, this is a memory enshrined in the biology of humanity. A lot like the human embryo remembers how to grow into a person (Freud, 1926/1991, p. 143; see also Haeckel, 1866, quoted in Dobzhansky, 1969, p. 17), collective memory is thought to be codified into the genetic make-up of a species.[34] Just like genes remember the physical characteristics of the ancestors of a person, an imprint is delivered on his or her mind, helping the individual to identify basic structures of meaning that are idiosyncratic to the culture and ethnicity the person comes from. The image below conveys graphically how this could be envisioned:

---

[33] Cf. the subtitle to Mary Shelley's Frankenstein: the modern Prometheus, referring to the hubris of a science that 'goes too far'.

[34] Sheldrake, by contrast, contended that there is no indication that a collective unconsciousness is codified in the human genes, and proposed his theory of a field of morphic resonance instead, in 'A New Science of Life' (1994, pp. 29-30 and 76-77).

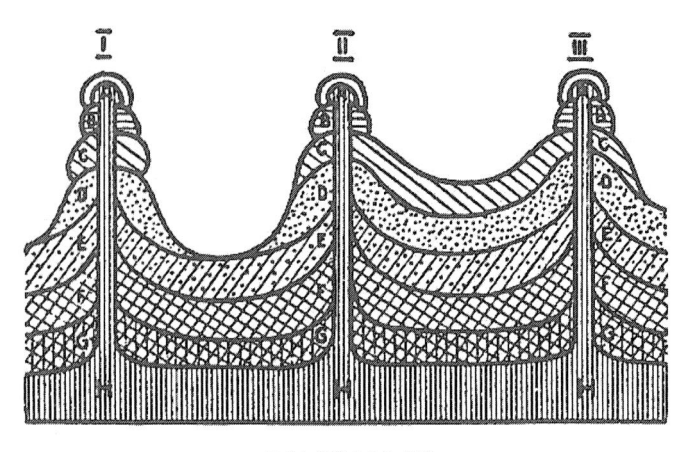

DIAGRAM XI

I. Single Nations.
II and III. Groups of Nations (e.g., Europe).
A. Individual.   E. Groups of People.
B. Family.   F. Primitive Human Ancestors.
C. Tribe.   G. Animal Ancestors.
D. Nation.   H. Central Force.

Figure 1 *Jung's architecture of the mind, according to Jacobi, 1949.*

For Jung, collective unconsciousness is a type of memory of humankind, similar to instincts, which helps human beings recognise forms, shapes or patterns 'by nature' rather than through conscious thoughts. Such patterns – archetypes – constitute cultural forms of recognition, for example, the 'innocent young girl' or the 'old wise man'. These are shapes that appear in myths and stories around the world, with seemingly universal meanings, thereby suggesting that the meanings associated with these characters are not culturally distinctive, but commonly human. This could suggest a biological origin or refer to the interface of culture and biology. Or, as Freud expressed this:

> Al was u dan geneigd te veronderstellen dat alles wat de psychoanalyse over de vroege seksualiteit van kinderen vertelt, aan de tomeloze fantasie van de analytici ontsproten is, u kunt toch tenminste toegeven dat deze fantasie dezelfde voortbrengselen heeft geschapen als de fantasiewerkzaamheid van de primitieve mensheid, waar mythen en sprookjes de neerslag van

zijn. De andere, minder onvriendelijke en waarschijnlijk ook juistere opvatting zou luiden dat in het zieleleven van het kind nu nog steeds dezelfde archaïsche krachten kunnen worden aangetoond die eens, in de oertijden van de menselijk cultuur, algemeen geheerst hebben. Het kind zou dan in zijn psychische ontwikkeling de geschiedenis van de stam in verkorte vorm herhalen, zoals de embryologie dat al lang voor de lichamelijke ontwikkeling heeft onderkend (1926/1991, p. 143).

Even though you might have tended to assume that all that psychoanalysis has to say about the early sexuality of children is born from the uncontrolled phantasy of the analysts, you could at least admit that this phantasy has brought about the same products as the phantastic activities of primitive humanity, which myths and fairy tales are the results of. The other, less unfriendly and probably also more correct conception would be that in the mental life of the child the same archaic forces can still be demonstrated to be at work that once, in the original times of human culture, reigned generally. The child would then in its psychological development repeat the history of the tribe in a shortened form, just like embryology has recognised since long for physical development (1926/1991, p. 143).

What is important to note for our purpose is that, while time is paramount for conscious perception, in the (unconscious) memory, time plays a role of much smaller significance. There is an interesting parallel from the natural sciences (*in casu* geology) with this phenomenon, which is 'deep time'. Timescales of the unconsciousness seem surprisingly comparable to those of geology. Timescales of geology are completely different from those in (biological) evolution theory, which are again completely different from those of human experience, as Kroonenberg noted (2007, pp. 51-52). For human experience, 80 years is a lifetime. The human species as such, however, has been in existence for around 200,000 years (*homo sapiens*, rather than *homo erectus*, as the latter is thought to have existed for a million years approximately).

Jung said that, on an unconscious level, we are aware of the relativity of 'human time'. This awareness is ingrained in the mind. However, it is deeply hidden under the layers of consciousness, of sensory perceptions, which are coming to the mind at a much faster pace, and which, in our media-governed world that itself suggests a high-paced existence and change of public consciousness almost by the minute, one can hardly escape from. Indeed, Western society, and increasingly societies in general, seems to celebrate stimuli, which suggests an obstacle to experiencing the depths of our mind, which requires the absence, rather than presence of stimuli as Schopenhauer said (1818/1996, p. 280). Time becomes more relative, i.e. its significance decreases, the more one descends into the mind (descends, as per Jung's model in the figure above): from the here and now of perception to the tens of years in which a human being forms her or his ideas of life as a whole, and their life itself, to the tens of thousands of years in which our peoples and tribes have differentiated from the main species and, before that, how our species itself came into existence. One may even imagine that, following the lines of Jung's theory, the Big Bang – the moment in which time itself started – is ingrained in our minds. However, to unearth it would require some real psychological 'archaeology'.

In the schema in Fig. 1 above, the most fundamental layer represents the origin of the mind, i.e. of perception and of time, and therefore, indeed, of everything. It is not a coincidence that, while consciousness is ruled by time in a very direct sense, or as per Kant, consciousness and time are identical, Jacobi equated this fundamental dimension with eternity. Where time plays an ever more relative role the deeper one descends into the mind, it ceases to play a role at all in its deepest layers, where we find the unchanged and unchangeable or, to use a religious expression, that what is, was and always will be. This is a very interesting realm, not only because of its many implications for human existence in a greater order of things but also because it has been known to several philosophers by several names: it was known to Plato as the Oneness that is the reality behind the manifoldness of sensory perception, which he described in the Republic; to the Italian-German bishop Nicolaus Cusanus as the *coincidentia oppositorum* or point of convergence of opposites, which he described in his main work *De docta ignorantia* (see 1440/1954); and to Kant, who knew this realm as the source of pure knowledge or home of the *Dinge an sich*. Kant's Vernunft represents the faculty of the human being that has access to this realm and of which by virtue of their Vernunft, and therewith humanity,[35] each human being is a part.

However, it was of course consciousness that discovered unconsciousness, as well as eternity, and not the other way around. It is the contrast created by the existence of these two, dissimilar worlds (one, which is time and the other one where time does not exist) that is remarkable. It is the operation of that other world, beyond time, in the shared world of the here and now, which does not fail to give rise to fascination, for example when it works through intuition, that is to say, the manifest establishment of a connection between these realms. The artist at work, converting inspiration into a work with 'an idea'; or the researcher, devising hypotheses. Intuition and intelligence may be closer to one another than might be expected. So then eternity is not 'infinite time' but absence of time or, as Wittgenstein said in Thesis 6:4311 of his '*Tractatus logic-philosophicus*', eternity is timelessness (1969, p.81). The fact that for consciousness this is not imaginable, results in a paradox. The mentioned coincidentia oppositorum, devised by Nicolaus Cusanus (also called De Cusa), may well be the best description of this in philosophical terms. In *De visione dei*, Cusanus described the place where God is found as follows: "'Now' and 'then' are obstacles halfway on the road of who goes towards Thou: in the wall that marks the place where Thou resideth in coincidence. 'Now' and 'then' coincide in the circle that is the wall of paradise" (1453/1993, p. 74). Paradise, here, is understood as eternity.

To illustrate this mathematically, Cusanus explained that, while quantities (number) can be expressed of all things that are capable of comparison, this is not the case with infinity, which is therefore, by definition, unknown (p. 8). As it is the maximum, however, which includes everything, Cusanus concluded that it must be unity, which is God (p.

---

[35] Incidentally, Kant did not say that only human beings can have Vernunft.

9). This maximum, which is unity of all things and is therefore 'no thing' in particular is, due to this fact, in the same time the absolute minimum (p. 13). In as far as the human mind is unable to grasp the identity of the minimum and the maximum, Cusanus speaks of 'learned ignorance', arguing that the absolute truth is beyond our human grasp (p. 10). Certainly, proceeding to truth "through the things made known to us by nature" (i.e. as the natural sciences do) "falls very far short" of this as it is not capable of conveying knowledge of the maximum (p. 13). Cusanus supported this idea by quoting Rabbi Salomon, who claimed that the Creator is not apprehended by the sciences (p. 35).

Cusanus attempted to illustrate this idea geometrically. For example, he argued that a line of a measure of an infinite number of feet is not different in distance than a line of an infinite number of lengths of two feet (p. 36). Oddly, Cusanus also argued, with reference to a polygon of equal sides that, the greater the number of sides in this polygon, the more the figure starts to look like a circle but that it would never become a circle (p. 11). While it would be difficult to prove this, the rest of Cusanus' argument actually suggests the opposite, i.e. that if the number of sides is infinite, the figure becomes a circle – i.e. a figure without any angles. While not overly significant, this points to another issue in Cusanus' theory. In Chapter V, Cusanus argued that the maximum cannot be a number, in Chapter X, he argued that the maximum is one (p. 24). This seems in line with his idea that it is unity. However, one may also argue that the maximum and minimum coincide in zero, rather than one, which is not necessarily a natural number. This could be understood from the perspective that the number of angles of the above-mentioned figure (zero) would return to zero when it became infinite. Moreover, it would clarify why Denys the Great (as quoted by Cusanus, p. 39) said that "an understanding of God is not so much an approach towards something as towards nothing" adding that "sacred ignorance teaches me that what seems nothing to the intellect is the incomprehensible Maximum." It is here, in nothing, that opposites coincide, in a similar fashion to how the opposites of consciousness coincide in unconsciousness and, to an even greater extent, in eternity.

The human mind, briefly, consists of these two extremes: consciousness, which does not just exist in the here and now, but is it (i.e. it is this specific shape of time) and eternity. It is this tension, this inherent paradox revealing itself as intrinsic problem of the human condition: the *Mittelwesen* (intermediary being) of Heinisch (1960, p. 235); the absurdity of being of Camus (2013, p. 111, 169); the status quo of the post-modern condition; and the place between animal and angel in some classical taxonomies of beings,[36] such as where St. Augustine (426/2007, p. 422) said:

> Zo is de mens bijvoorbeeld een soort wezen in het midden, maar dan tussen de dieren en de engelen. Een dier is een niet-redelijk en sterfelijk levend wezen, een engel een redelijk en onsterfelijk levend wezen. De mens staat daar midden tussenin, lager dan de engelen en hoger dan de dieren; hij is een redelijk en sterfelijk levend wezen, dat zijn sterfelijkheid met de dieren, zijn redelijkheid met de engelen gemeen heeft.

> So then the human being is, for example, a kind of being in the middle, but between the animals and the angels. An animal is a non-reasonable and mortal being, an angel a reasonable and immortal being. The human being is located between these two, lower than angels and higher than animals; he is a reasonable and mortal living being, who has its mortality in common with animals, his reason with the angels.

An intuition of this split, and its nature, between an existence in the here and now and eternity or timelessness, is much older than any of these sources, however: Plato wrote that the real philosopher should not become involved in politics, as long as his utopia (The Republic) is not realised (4th century BCE/1995a, p. 243); similarly, St. Augustine referred to a City of God that exists in eternity, while the city of the earth (Babel, Rome) exists in the here and now (426/2007, p. 43). The city of eternity is, of course, superior according to St. Augustine. Even

---

[36] For an example, see Garrett's webpage Hierarchy ethics and enlightenment ethics (2004, point 4), retrieved 10 November 2007 from http://www.wku.edu/~jan.garrett/320/hierenlt.htm.

Schopenhauer (1818/1996, II, p. 472) said, albeit providing a completely different perspective, that:

> Das Individuum wurzelt in der Gattung und die Zeit in der Ewigkeit: und wie jeglisches Individuum dies nur dadurch ist, daß es das Wesen seiner Gattung an sich hat; so hat es auch nur dadurch zeitliche Dauer, daß es zugleich in der Ewigkeit ist.

> The individual is rooted in the species and time in eternity: and how every individual only is one because it has the essence of the species; so does its existence in time [its temporality] only exist due to that the fact that it simultaneously exists in eternity.

At this point, we can recognise that the tension, which Richard Rorty identified as the root of all philosophy, has the same, or at least a similar genealogy to the one that is the root of all religion: in universals, we recognise a counterpart to our time of eternity; in particulars, the perception in the here and now. And it is thus that reality manifests itself to us. It is this unresolved tension within us, at the heart of our identities and existence in the world, that makes us turn to philosophy, or religion, to understand the reality of things. Indeed, Heidegger (1927/2006) already saw that time functions as a criterion for what he called the naïve distinction between different realms of Being: "A 'temporal' Being (the occurrences in nature and the events of history) is distinguished from a 'non-temporal' Being (spatial and numerical relations). … Furthermore, a 'gap' is found between the 'temporal' Being and the 'over-temporal' eternity and an attempt is made to bridge this" (p. 18). An understanding of this basic notion that the human being lives in two worlds or times simultaneously helps us look at the history of philosophy in an entirely new light. For example, Hooykaas identified the problem of being and becoming as the main problem of ancient Greek philosophy in general: how, philosophers wondered, can something that was not already the case, come to be (1976, p. 20)? Zeno's paradox 'The Flying Arrow Stands Still' refers to precisely this question. In this paradox, an arrow flies, and as such it is said to be in a place but, if it really were in a place, why would it not fall down (Goedegebuure 1986, p. 77)?

From our newly acquired perspective, we can formulate an answer to this question: we can say that stillness – being in a place - in nature, that is all that is subject to perception,[37] does not exist. In Schopenhauer's words (1818/1996, I, p. 220): "So as every [physical] body has to be seen as the manifestation of a will, while will necessarily reflects a striving; thus the original situation of any earth shaped as a bullet cannot be stillness, but has to be movement, striving forward in infinite space, without rest or end goal." The idea of stillness in nature, it seems, is the result of the encounter of our perception of nature, and the concept of stillness, which originates in our minds, and is perceived into, rather than in, nature. Here, we see that our initial set of dichotomies – chiefly, physical versus metaphysical - overlaps with at least one additional one: the first dimension, of the physical, is identified with time, therefore transient and in constant movement; the second one, of the metaphysical, is identified as somehow outside of time, or eternal, and still. The inherently paradoxical essence of the human condition lies in that it does not belong just to either of these domains but consists of the encounter of these dimensions.

Now, for our purpose, it is of importance to observe that *the institutional resolution of this paradox is religion*. Therefore religion is related to the very root of our inherently paradoxical existence. We may try to escape from this paradoxical root of our existence, for example, by seeking stimuli such as surfing Internet, attending parties, overwork, i.e. do everything possible to retreat into the here and now, or into our consciousness with its noise and other stimuli, but we cannot make it disappear. Still, modern society aims at precisely that: it generates a constant flux of information and, more in general, a constant exposure to sensory impressions. Possibly the strongest case in point is the television: television is a continuous feed of images to the mind, resulting in a potential addiction that makes the aforementioned 'way of omission' so difficult to achieve that one would almost say the destination it leads to, does altogether not exist. With Plato, and also with the Catholic Church,

---

[37] Kant's definition of nature was that it is all that operates under laws, differently from human consciousness, which operates on the basis of freedom, given to it by the moral law.

the mentioned dichotomies overlapped with a third one: good and evil. For Plato, the real and therefore good world was the metaphysical one. Similarly, for the Catholic Church, the human condition has long been represented as one in exile; of an ethereal spirit in a physical world subject to time, and therefore, to rot. In the words of Le Goff (1988), speaking of the Middle Ages: "God's incarnation was also his humiliation. The body was an *ergastulum*, a slave's prison for the soul" (p. 83).

Even so, in the view of 19th century rabbi Abraham Geiger, Christianity still was an inferior religion to Judaism "since the doctrine of the Incarnation [of God in Jesus] compromises the original purity of the Jewish concept of God" (Cohn-Sherbok, 2007, p. 75). For 16th century kabbalist Isaac Luria, Adam, the first-mentioned human being in the Bible, symbolically representing the dualism in the cosmos, "possessed a sacred soul while his body represented the evil forces" (id., p. 132). In a similar vein, in Hinduism, the physical world is 'maya' or temporary illusion. Analogous to how the human condition is neither only the physical, nor only the metaphysical, nor only the flesh or only the spirit, as it were, but the encounter of both, while the natural sciences on occasion purport to be the sciences of the physical, they really operate on the interface of these two worlds (this is why Edith Stein was also right when she said that, in spite of the duality mentioned above, the human being is not a *Doppelwesen*, 2009, p. 407). They do not consist of abstract concepts alone (that is to say those that relate to Schopenhauer's Vernunft, which is itself based on Kant's Vernunft), but neither are they informed only by direct perception (or Schopenhauer's Verstand, see 1818/1996, p. 97) – they are concepts applied to perception. In that sense, science is an inherently human activity.

For something – some thing - to be perceived, it has to be finite. If something has no boundaries, it transcends all things, and thus becomes imperceptible. It is for this reason that, whereas the realm of the metaphysical or abstract factually exists, it cannot be empirically perceived. It is in line with this idea that, for example, the Qur'an says that God contains everything (Sura An Nisa (4), Aya 127) and that eyes cannot reach Him (Sura Al An'aam (6), Aya 104). For perception, and for the sciences of perception (i.e. the natural sciences), eternity, as discussed above, cannot exist. This clearly marks their limitation.[38] An example, or parable, to clarify this further: if, in the empirical world, there existed just two colours, blue and red, we would imagine that two colours existed. We would be able to think in terms of colour and distinguish these from one another. However, if one of these colours disappeared, then we could not say that one colour remains. We would say that no colour is left, as there is no difference or counterfactual against which the existence of a colour as such could be established. Moreover, the concept of colour itself would disappear or, as Edith Stein (2009, p. 50) wrote:

> That there can be no color without being red or blue or green is what is distinctive of genuine specification.

Therefore, if something is in everything and everywhere, eternally, all-pervading, we cannot perceive it. That alone, however, does not mean that it does not exist. What happens is that it moves from the 'here and now' to the time of eternity. Therefore, numerically expressed, we would have to agree with Plato in that the real miracle is not how something can come from nothing (part of what Dobzhansky called the *mysterium tremendum*, 1969, p. 25), although this was formulated by Wittgenstein as a major philosophical question (1969, p. 81) in Thesis 6.44 of his 'Tractatus logico-philosophicus' (mystical is not *how* the world is, but *that* it is); it is how manifoldness can spring from unity. As a consequence, it is not the step from zero to one that interests us, but how one can be both one (conceptually and for unconsciousness) and zero (for the natural sciences or the conscious mind). The answer lies, I believe, in the relation between structure and content or, otherwise formulated, in the notion that structure creates content. Structure itself cannot be perceived, although and possibly because of the fact that it is all-pervasive, but it assigns content its place in time, which, when it has been assigned its place – and only then – can be perceived. This analysis suggests that consciousness, fundamentally, has a narrative structure: at

---

[38] As written in an article in Gamma (Bilagher 2006, p. 42-44): in addition to all of its considerable merits.

the bottom of it is meaning. Its elements, experiences, emanate from it, but they could not exist without a greater structure tying them together.

This is a basic idea in Paul Ricoeur's *Temps et Récit*. According to Ricoeur, stories in essence consist of a *mise en intrigue*, somewhat like a plot, which assigns its separate parts their places (1983, p. 102). To illustrate this, refer to the following example of a story consisting of two scenes (Bilagher, 2005, with some modifications):

> a man slaps a child in the face; 2. the child is hysterically crying. If we read these events in this sequence [1, 2], we would have the understanding of a 'story' where a man beats a child and the child cries because it is hurt. In this sequence [1, 2], which we could call act 1, scene 1 (the slap) is probably not very pleasant. However, if we change the order of the events to [2, 1] both obtain a diametrically opposed meaning: in this case we could read that the child has an attack of hysteria, which the man tries to cure by slapping it. The slap turns from 'bad' to 'good' – not because the slap itself changes, or because any scenes are added or deleted, but simply because of a permutation of the existing material.

Another illustration of the same idea, in the form of a joke:[39]

> A salesman of a certain softdrink returns from his Middle East assignment. A friend asks him: "Why weren't you successful with the Arabs?" The salesman explained: "When I got posted in the Middle East, I was very confident that I will make a good sales pitch. But I had a problem: I didn't speak Arabic. So I planned to convey the message through 3 posters: in the first poster, a man is crawling through the hot desert sand, totally exhausted. In the second one, the man is drinking our drink, and thirdly, our man is completely refreshed. Then these posters were posted all over the place." "That should have worked," said the friend. The salesman replied, "well, not only did I not

---

[39] This is mentioned in the same article, but it is not its source, which, although widely diffused, is unknown to me.

speak Arabic, I also didn't realize that Arabs read from right to left..."

This indicates how we could think, in my view, of what is at the fundament of our minds, which is eternity and, according to many or even all religions, our Creator (Stein already suggested that "we may call eternal being 'Creator'", 2009, p. 71). Our Creator is meaning. Meaning makes experience possible and, therefore, creates reality (as earlier). As a consequence, we can be assured that we will be able to find meaning in seemingly unconnected, meaning-deprived and random occurrences in our daily realities. This is the 'good news', or *evangelos*, of religion. This is our continuation of Kant's Copernican revolution: reality does not start with the atomic elements of reality, but with the patterns that emerge from it. The pattern, meaning, was here first (or, as Cusanus would say, the Word preceded the 'now' and 'then' that represent conscious experience). However, in our human condition of exile, the rules our mind has set up for itself[40] entail that we believe things to be exactly the other way around than they actually are: we start to think from the concrete, earthly, and believe that this can lead us to the realms of abstractness – normally imagined as the sky or heavens. This is considered 'common sense'. As Jewish Andalusian 12th century philosopher Ibn Daud contended, the "common people assume that what is not matter does not exist" (Cohn-Sherbok, 2007, p. 48).

Incidentally, from the thesis that our Creator is meaning, it does not follow that our Creator is impersonal. Indeed we, as persons, can well be understood as exponents of meaning – but our conscious experience is contingent upon our individuality, because we can only perceive meaning – in time and space – as part of a sequence and not as an integral, immanent whole.

---

[40] As discussed earlier, Rorty described Kant's contribution to philosophy as a shift from enquiry into the original nature of knowledge to one into the rules the mind had set up for itself.

The realm of the Prophets and the specificities of time

Our analysis has now led us to the hypothesis that there are two times existing alongside one another in the human mind: the here and now, in which we communicate, which is perceived as our normal, shared reality, in which our normal laws – natural and moral – hold; and that other one, in which time is either relative or non-existent, this non-linear world in which the laws that order our natural reality, those that are its basis[41] (the pillars of our consciousness), do not seem to apply. There may be an alarming element in the idea that there exists a realm where our normal, natural laws do not apply. Yet we will all be aware of the dream, literally our most daily encounter with that other world, which the Qur'an referred to when it said that God "takes one's spirit' in the night", in Sura al An'aam (6), Aya 61. In the dream, normal givens such as chronology, cause and effect and the consistency of space behave in a different way. Moreover, even moral laws may not play the same role in dreams as they do for consciousness. One may wake up, shocked at the thought that one has had a promiscuous dream or dreamt of doing something 'mad', dangerous or immoral.

In this context, it may be of interest to note that the division between moral and natural laws, as we know it now, has not always existed. Kwa argued that originally "[t]he notion 'natural law'" expressed "that nature has to conform to laws, which are formulated by a Divine Legislator." Observing that the Old Testament contains several passages to this effect (Job 38:10, Psalms 104:9, Proverbs 8:29 and Jeremiah 5:22), Kwa noted that while these natural laws did not add up to a codification comparable to the Ten Commandments, they were apparently meant to be analogous to them. Thus, he said, we can speak of a metaphor: "nature has to conform to laws, just like human beings have to" (1991, p. 108). Only in the 17th century, Kwa concluded, i.e. during the scientific revolution, did the paths of ethics and science go into separate

---

[41] As said in Footnote 38, for Kant, nature in general is everything operating under laws (1974, p. 156). We find this idea in Kwa (1991, p. 110), indirectly, where he said that for Francis Bacon nature is everything that can be forced to obey to him, as if he were an inquisitor, and thereby shows being subject to the law.

directions (*idem*, p. 109).

Although the greatest parts of our lives take place in the world of physical perception, and thus consciousness, the intuition of an 'existence of something else' is often there, even if only through the awareness of the finitude of life. Traditionally, there have been persons mediating between these worlds we inhabit. Such mediators were historically called prophets or shamans. Prophets were those people that were able to dig into the depths of their souls, to find a concept or tool in the realms were time would not enter and apply this to practical situations in the 'real' world. According to David Goldberg and John Rayner, in Judaism, prophets are persons inspired by God (1989, pp. 38-40). Here, with inspiration, I understand to be meant operating under the influence of the other world. Prophets were regarded as people of vision: this referred specifically and, one may say, ironically, not to a clear vision of empirical reality but, almost on the contrary, to an ability to see beyond it. In this sense, vision is an ability to go beyond the 'here and now' and imagine possibilities, usually for a better world, or even a utopia. For example, in a speech in Memphis, Tennessee, on 3 April 1969, the night before he was assassinated, Martin Luther King said:

> I just want to do God's will. And He's allowed me to go up to the mountain. And I've looked over. And I've seen the promised land.

To the 19th century rabbi Samson Rafael Hirsch, prophecy did not denote an ability to foresee a future in the sense of simple divination (1842, p. 605). Rather, it denoted the ability to see the ideal future of mankind (id., p. 604). While this applied to King's vision, it was also the kind of prophecy that Popper criticised (in particular in the case of Marx): the idea of historicism, that is to say, that a future, which is seen by the prophet, must materialise. According to Popper (2006, p. 455), one of the earliest forms of historicism is found in the notion that the Jewish people are the chosen people in a story of which the author is Jahweh and of which the Biblical prophets asserted to be able to see the future. One may write a human history of imagined futures, to understand the times they were conceived in, ranging from an ever-deteriorating quality of life from the Golden Times, with Hesiod, via eschaton and the end of times to the inevitability of communism, dystopia and the encounter with extra-terrestrial life or aliens as in the 1990s television series 'The X-files'.

It may be fair to say that the role of the prophet in ancient times is similar to that of the intellectual in present society (Bilagher, 2010). The intellectual distinguishes him- or herself from regular persons of science in that that he or she does not only pursue (academic) knowledge and understanding, but also actively participates in the political debates of their societies. Like the prophet unites the unchanging principles of the metaphysical world with the questions and challenges of their present time, in order to produce practical solutions based on unchanging principles, the intellectual applies concepts and ideas from the world of knowledge with the practical, political, social and economic issues of the day. As Goldberg and Rayner said of prophets:

> They are all interpreters of current events in the light of general religious and moral principles. They are all, in varying degrees, critics of contemporary society, fearless in delivering their message, however unpopular it may be. (1989, p. 199)

Both intellectuals and prophets, therefore, unite our two worlds or, rather, our two times of the here and now and eternity. This is of course not in line with the thought of those who believe that prophets are people of the past. Even if unconsciously, this does not seem to be a very unusual understanding. For example, Magris observed (2018, p. 233) that no one seemed to be surprised or shocked that the relatively recently established, oecumenical Baha'i religion is currently not permitted in the Islamic Republic of Iran:

> … maybe because its origin is so recent and we sense the sanctity of religions only when they are enveloped by an aura of antiquity, of remote times, and do not believe that new Revelations may occur in an epoch close to us – even if the temporal distance between Abraham and today, with respect to the age

or even just the history of the world, is very brief, an instant as regards millennia.

The timeless world is the world of the abstract; the world of time (i.e. consciousness) that of the concrete. The timeless world is a world of reflection; the world of time, of action. And so on: many of the constituent tensions of human existence originate in this initial dichotomy of times of which, as mentioned, religion has traditionally been the attempt at a shared, institutional resolution. Dobzhansky was certainly right when he said that an "urge to devise answers to such 'metaphysical' questions is a part of the psychological equipment of the human species" (1969, p. 4), quoting Brinton (1953) saying that:

> Metaphysics is a human drive or appetite, and to ask men (sic) to do without metaphysics is as pointless as to ask them to do without sex relations.

However, while this dichotomy, this tension and urge may be the source of human freedom, a misunderstanding of this origin of religion can lead to a significant reduction in this same freedom. For this reason, understanding this dialectical split and, as a consequence, 'how the mind is set up' is not only of academic interest. After all, this duality in our minds does not only influence how we see and understand reality (it seems, to an extent, un-understandable and paradoxical) but also motivates us to do certain things and, first of all, given our difficulty in tolerating ambiguity, find some kind of resolution. In going about this, we undertake to have the mind, using philosophy as an instrument to explore the nature of perception, understand itself to a greater extent. In this examination, we have so far observed that consciousness equates, to a large extent, with time and that time has a direction, stipulated by structure. But this structure is not only a generic structure. It is also a specific structure, which suggests it has a shape, for example, linear or circular. One of the assumptions we have, in any case, is that time goes forward. A non-conformistic thought was suggested by Umberto Eco in 'Foucault's Pendulum': that time goes backward rather than forward (1999, p. 213). In this work, the character Agliè says:

Modern thought says that time is a linear and purposive sequence going from A to B. Time can also go from B to A, then effect follows from cause… […] Does your beautiful Amparo come before or after her ancestors? She is too magnificent – if you have no objection against the objective judgement of someone who could have been her father. She therefore precedes them. She is the mysterious source that has contributed to create her.

What is of interest here is not whether time really goes either forward or backward; what is of interest is to re-emphasise that time and meaning intersect. In Eco's example, the seemingly neutral entity of time – a witness of events – is used to provide a value judgement through the concept of an origin. Meaning or justification is sometimes found in an origin, at a beginning, as in the case of the justification for the claim of the Jewish people to the land of Israel, where it is based on the Biblical book Deuteronomy. But who says that the origin is a more legitimate ground for a claim than other possible options, such as the present or future? Does the past have more meaning than the future? Like Agliè argued that the direction of time may also be from B to A, legitimacy of actions may depend on the future as well. For example, the existence of the country of the Netherlands, although certainly an artificial construction, can be justified with a reference to a future situation where this provision, i.e. the state, will contribute to the well-being of its citizens, in the first place, without disregarding due rights of others.

For this reason, it is probably not a coincidence that it was the great Triestine writer Claudio Magris, whose work focused on the encounter of national identities and who is one of the fathers of 'border literature', who emphasised that it was Nietzsche who taught us that, where one's origins lie is ultimately unimportant (2001a, p. 347). In line with Toulmin's idea that philosophers are influenced by problems they perceive in their environment, Magris was weary of the 'politics of identity' that have traditionally been so important in Central Europe (2018, p. 164, 254). Trieste is not only a point of encounter between Germanic, Romance and Slavic culture in Europe, but has also been part of different States in the course of its history. It is therefore probably with hope that Magris said, in his novel Danube (2001a, p. 252) that the "past has a future, something it becomes, and that transforms it" – i.e. events in the future change the past, or at least, the perception of it. By contrast, the prevailing understanding of reality in the Middle Ages had been that since the creation of humanity, there had not been a substantial change in how human beings lived and that there had been no real development. According to Debora Meijers, for example, until the 19th century, a point in time was considered to be like a spatial coordinate on a geographical map (1991). Magris' thought seems to speak of the hope that we can, in the future, find a past that belongs to all of us and that does not assign specific pieces of land to specific groups of people because their origin, their genesis and not that of others, can allegedly be found there.

This transformation of the past itself relies on the ability of consciousness, or time, to reflect on itself, because it is the same as the ability to see unity in manifoldness. Namely, 'pure' consciousness would only be living in the here and now, without reflection and without an understanding of where the here and now, and its perception of it, come from; the ability to see unity in manifoldness is the ability to draw the separate experiences in consciousness – manifoldness – into a meaningful whole, or unity or sequence in time (which we could call a history or narrative, as mentioned before). This is possible in as far as consciousness has a conception of non-time, or an origin or future – end of time – when there was no time yet, and unity, and is capable of perceiving its contents through that lens. This suggests that Plato interpreted intelligence correctly: as the ability of any person to see unity in manifoldness (4th century BCE/1995a, p. 144). This consists on one level of the ability to perceive the structure that unites concrete and tangible entities (for example, the concept and the object of chair) and, on another level, of understanding of the fundamental unity of things and recognise a separate dimension beyond the world of appearances.

In a similar vein, Stein (2009, p. 129) would say that:

Acts that conceive something else, grasping it in its order and connectedness and treating it in accordance with its order, are analogous to divine wisdom and reason.

The religiously minded reader, and possibly the Muslim reader in particular, will think of the difference between polytheism (manifoldness) and monotheism (unity) now; and the Catholic one, in particular, of St. Augustine's case for monotheism against the multiple gods of the Roman pantheon in the 'City of God' (e.g. 426/2007, pp. 198-199). More directly, the atheist mind is similar to the polytheist one: she or he sees the manifold manifestations in nature but does not see what unites these. Similarly, it may see the different origins, which divide different groups, but not the one origin, which unites these groups. Crucially, they may even see different religions, but not religion, for what it is. Therefore, understanding (mono-) theism requires a certain type of intelligence, related to the ability of abstraction.[42] Deity, one might say, is the ultimate abstraction. It is not in sense perception but underlies or precedes it. It is, as several religious Books say, at the beginning of time and will be at the end of time. Its perception is therefore not a given, but depends on the ability of the individual for it to be recognised; an ability, which is subjective, that is to say dependent on the subject, in as far as she or he is able to see unity in manifoldness or 'intelligent'. This suggests that intelligence is at least in part reflected by the extent to which one manages to integrate and solve the mentioned inherent human paradox, that is, the existence on the verge between the here and now of consciousness and a timeless dimension at the bottom of the mind (eternity),[43] where all is One and, therefore, the extent to which one manages to apply the conceptual instruments from this abstract world in empirical reality.

One may argue that this reflects the extent to which we have access to a certain part of our minds, which we have all in common but may

---

[42] According to Howard Gardner (2011), there does not exist only one intelligence, but there are multiple intelligences.
[43] Stein referred to a 'substance' at the bottom of our temporal experience (2009, p. 17).

not have equal access to. This is the part of our minds that we access through prayer or meditation (the 'Central Force' in Fig. 1), or the realm of the prophets as mentioned earlier. It is non-local: it is the *coincidentia oppositorum* of minds into the Mind from which the ideas and concepts that are used in and applied to the empirical world, originate. This is one of two main reasons that explain why we, as a human species, share concepts. The other reason is that these concepts are true and as human beings we all have access to truth (although the extent to which this is the case may depend on our intelligence). We cannot imagine the existence of anything without this Mind and, as such, this is the Creator of everything. It creates our reality because, on the one hand, in one way or another, it enables our existential individuality, while, on the other, it gives us (abstract) instruments to make sense of it, and in that sense, makes it what it is. In that regard, it is identical to the meaning unfolding itself in and through our consciousness, mentioned earlier. In line with this, Stein argued that ideas come from eternity (2009, p. 107).

This line of reasoning implies that artificial intelligence (AI), which has no access to Mind, is a *contradictio in terminis* (Bilagher, 2008). As detailed above, intelligence is, in essence, a movement from the general (or conceptual, abstract) to the particular (empirical, concrete) or specific. As a consequence, it operates on the verge of the two realms of which the tension, according to Rorty, has given rise to the history of philosophy as know it. Intelligence originates in the Platonic unity and refers, in essence, to an application or recognition of this unity in the world of consciousness, through which humanity is able to order and make sense of the world. Artificial intelligence, on the other hand, is by definition unable to do that as its thinking fundamentally starts from building blocks (bits, 0s and 1s), building up to structures envisioned by the human mind. With reference, once more, to the entity of time, for a computer, that other, timeless reality does not exist, as it cannot be part of it. It can obey to human intelligence, but not be intelligent itself.

This idea seems to be in line with classical theory from the field of educational psychology, which holds that analysis, synthesis and evaluation are so-called higher order thinking skills, while memorisation and reproduction belong to the category of lower order skills, in the taxonomy of Bloom et al. (1956/1984). Indeed, memorisation focuses on concrete instances, such as specific words and, for example, their translation into another language. Synthesis requires the assembly and ordering of such instances into greater unities of meaning, such as reordering a set of words in such a way that they obtain a new meaning or expression. Some components of traditional IQ tests focus on this ability as well: to recognise patterns, trends and regularities in series of data points. To be able to conduct a synthetic operation, it may be that one should already have a vision of its outcome, after which the parts that fit the concerning requirement are selected. The mind temporarily goes 'out of time' (it looks into the future or, more precisely, enters the time of eternity) to the final, desired outcome, and then comes 'back to time' (i.e. comes back to the here and now) to realise the sequential steps – *in concreto* or abstractly – to arrive at the envisioned outcome.

The operation of analysis is clearly different. It enables the reader to look at texts on different levels, and with different instruments and perspectives in mind. One such method lies in identifying dichotomies, which could reveal hidden presuppositions and ideological positions of the authors of a text. This is what I will turn to now: to take a look at religious text and see how, from the perspective that belief is the ability to see unity in manifoldness, or abstraction, they speak to us.

The rethinking of religion

My contention is that the idea that the human condition is essentially based on its existence in two times can fundamentally change our vision on religion. Whereas religion, or what it refers to, is at times ridiculed as standing above the laws of nature, it is revealing itself to be at the roots of nature's laws. Religion does not stand above nature in the sense that regularities in nature can be transgressed by it (such as a man rising from the dead, within the time of consciousness), but changes the way we conceive of nature: nature is, on one hand, the substance of conscious perception, i.e. the time of the here and now, but on the other hand the laws governing the events in this perception. It consists of physics (natural phenomena) and metaphysics (the framework in which these fit or the laws governing these phenomena). In as far as metaphysics precede physics, and religion is the domain of the metaphysical while nature is that of the physical, it does stand above nature.

There is therefore no contradiction between science and religion. Consciousness is the realm of science; the realm of religion is the 'other world' or, because we cannot 'think away' our consciousness, the domain of the relation between our consciousness and that other world or, formulated alternatively again, the resolution of the tension between our intuition of eternity and the acute awareness of our limited existence in the framework of time and place. There is nothing counter-natural about religion, therefore, and anything that is alleged to be may tentatively be asked to be associated with the realm of superstition. In that sense, it seems fair to refer to the worlds of science and religion as 'non-overlapping magisteria', as per the biologist Stephen Jay Gould (1997). According to Gould, science addresses empirical reality, while religion addresses morality. Apart from whether one agrees with this specific formulation, one may acknowledge that there remain areas of life for which science, at least apparently, does not provide us with relevant knowledge or only in the most indirect, not necessarily useful way. This relates to questions such as: how do I find happiness? Where should I place my priorities in life? How should I conceive of my relation to myself? Why does life seem to be finite and, if I die, do I disappear? What consequences should this have for my life choices?

On the basis of my argument so far, the notion that the counter-natural does not exist, does not mean that we should discard of religion. On the contrary. Nevertheless, because religion as a general phenomenon seems, at times, to have been hijacked by specific instances of it, namely by religions, I do see a need for it to be democratised. This should happen, mainly, for the simple reason that this may be the most secure safeguard against abuse of religious authority. However, while in science there are rules for the evaluation of hypotheses, within religion there currently are not. Through my preceding argument, and what follows, I hope to begin to devise a framework that may help address this lacuna. Thus, religion has to be newly explained. One of the most direct examples of what a new understanding of religion may look like can be derived from the reinterpretation of what it means to be a prophet, as discussed earlier on. Rather than someone endowed with access to the counter-natural, he or she is endowed with a particular access to the metaphysical realm or intelligence in the Platonic sense or vision, which enables this person to see beyond the here and now and interpret unchangeable truths with relevance to a particular situation. This gives guidance to us, ethically, in a broad sense, living in the world of consciousness.

One way in which this reinterpretation may work in practice, relevant to our discussion on time, may be clarified by means of the concepts of values and norms. A value is something which, if not unchangeable, is fairly constant, and which societies consider to be important (valuable). Examples of this are politeness, honesty, friendship and faithfulness. While one cannot say that the prevalence of such values is universal across cultures, their presence seems to be. However, the way in which these values are expressed (i.e. through norms, normative standards for actual behaviour) is usually defined by particular conditions, most of which are culturally determined, where culture itself, at least in part, may also be perceived of as a response to nature, i.e. the specific context. For example, whereas in Europe it is usually considered polite to look someone in the eyes when conversing with them, in Japan, this is often thought of as rude, and it is instead polite to look down, in particular in interaction with a senior person. The same value, politeness, is thus being expressed in different ways depending upon context.

Similarly, in a religious context, prophets can suggest the use of a certain behaviour in one context, whereas it does not have to be assumed that this same behaviour would be desirable in another. In line with this, the Qur'an, for example, says that there is a decision for every period in Sura Ar Ra'ad (13), Aya 39 and even though promoting the idea that Islam is the only right religion, the Qur'an does not deny that religion is a reconciliation of eternal wisdom with local circumstances as several ayas point to other habits in different places, for example, Sura Al Hajj (22), Aya 35. The Catholic philosopher St. Augustine similarly said that there can be different regulations for different times and places:

> And I did not discern that justice, which is being served by the good and holy persons, has on a much more magnificent and elevated plan all her prescriptions simultaneously, and that she does not change in any way, while this justice does not give her regulations to these different times at once, but allocates to every time its own law (400/1985, p. 72).

Another important way in which to address a reinterpretation of religion lies in the re-reading of prophetic or religious text. As the location of their (i.e. the prophecies') origins in a different world suggests, it is hard to imagine that they can speak to us in a conventional language. If the world where they come from is not linear, the texts themselves may not be strictly composed logically. Logic, after all, is connected to the laws of causality of consciousness, religion with the connection between consciousness and the deeper layers of the mind. As a consequence, ideas in prophetic texts are often expressed metaphorically or allegorically. The fact of this specific character of religion, that it inhabits a somewhat wild and, possibly, dangerous territory, i.e. that of the depths of the mind, has not always had unequivocally positive connotations. Carl Jung already noted that a psychosis consists of a loss of a focal point in the mind – in such a case the mind is, effectively, swallowed up by multiple minds, or Mind, and its conscious function, i.e. its existence as an individual in the here and now is damaged. Thus, unconsciousness, where there exists no ego, takes over the mind. Schopenhauer had, over a 100 years earlier, already suggested that geniality and madness border one another (1818/1996, I, p. 272). That is why only a limited group of persons have been willing to access this territory: the prophets.

The fact that they contain metaphorical writings indicates that the Sacred Texts have, at times, to be approached through a metaphorical reading, which corresponds with the second level of religious experience, mentioned earlier. In this regard, it is interesting that the Qur'an says, in Sura Ali Imraan (3), Aya 7, that some of its verses must be interpreted metaphorically. As mentioned above, the New Testament contains similar instructions for use, for example in Paul's Letter to the Galatians (4: 21-31). This is particularly interesting in that it has been said that Islam is incapable of allegory; that in Islam only what is literally true can be right, as Anil Ramdas asserted in *NRC Handelsblad* of 22 November 2004. One of Islam's main objections against Christianity had been that it sees Jesus as a Son of God, as has for example been said in Sura Al Maidah (5), Aya 18. Strictly monotheistic as Islam is, this has been thought of as not acceptable. However, most or at least many Christians would themselves consider Jesus to be a son of God in a metaphorical sense, so it is dubious that this idea would go against the spirit of monotheism.

Naturally, what this allegorical expression denotes is that Jesus incarnates the ideals of our Creator. That is, the metaphysical ideals identified through religion find their realisation in the empirical world, the shared space of the here and now of conscious perception; but possibly no more than any other human could, potentially, incarnate these ideals. Rabbi Samuel Hirsch, for example, wrote that "[e]very Jew, for that matter every man, should be what Jesus was: that was the summons of every prophet. Every Jew and every man will become so; that is the promise of the Messianic hope" (1842, p. 728; quoted from Cohn-Sherbok 2007, p. 109). One point that has often been employed to argue against a literal reading of the Bible is that of the impossibility of the chronology of the Story of Creation, in which the world is created in only seven days. After all, as pointed out by the English scientist Thomas Burnet, it would be difficult to create anything in any number of days if day and night did not yet exist as measures of time (see also discussion above). According to Toulmin and Goodfield (1982, p. 58), Philo of Alexandria had already posed himself this question in the year 20 BCE.

What is interesting here, however, is how the intuition of the prophets revealed that the world was created in stages, rather than that creation had brought about everything in one single instant; and also, that the sequence of the stages of this story roughly coincides with what we now know to have been the stages of physical development and biological evolution. For example, that the human being is a recent appearance on the stage of the earth, and that the earth and seas have shaped before life could develop in it and on these surfaces (Kroonenberg 2007, p. 63). It seems almost as if the human mind possesses a 'pre-human memory' (a term to my knowledge first coined by the Netherlands author and psychologist Ronald Pino), as a reviewer of David E. Jones' book 'An instinct for dragons' once wrote (Simpson, 2003, p. 134) – a recollection of a time before we existed as human beings. In the case of Jones' book, this was understood to be a memory of dinosaurs, which has led to the elaboration of the mythical figure of the dragon. Once we take a closer look at the Story of Creation and similar stories in the Bible, and other Sacred Books, we discover many messages and signs for readers of any time, including ours.

Allegory as a form of reasoning may have been most popular in the Middle Ages: in essence, it explains one thing by showing how something similar works. The Bible contains several allegories, such as the story of a rich man who gave sums of money (Talents) to three of his servants (Luke 19: 12-26). One of them used the money to build a house; the second one used it to start a business; the third one decided to bury the money in the earth, so as to be able to give the money back if his employer asked for it. When the master or employer returned after some time, and asked his servants what they had done with the money he had given them, they explained this. The rich man allowed the first two servants to keep their money, and profits, as they had done something useful with it. However, the third servant was asked to give the money back, as he had left it, uselessly, in the earth. Naturally, in this case, the story itself is not the point. As with literary postmodernism, which understands that stories can be read at different levels, this story can be read at the level of the story – the level in which children might be interested in it, depending, of course, on the child – but it can also be read as having a meaning or several meanings. Catholicism itself identifies the literal reading; the allegorical one; the moral one; and the anagogical one.

Leaving these specific types of readings aside, one of the possible interpretations of the story is that money is not something that should be kept in the ground, but that should somehow 'roll'; that something should be done with it, as money in itself is nothing. Money should be invested, not necessarily consumed; and it can be used to generate a greater amount of money – if it is left stagnant, it does not remain, but disappears. In this account, the rich man seems to have represented the order of things (nature). Possibly, the concept of interest derives from this reading.[44] Another reading attributes allegorical – metaphorical – value to the money itself, saying that the sums of money represent talents, or human resources, which are given to people (represented by the servants) by their Creator. It then indicates the duty of persons to use their resources instead of saving them up. That is to say, if one is given an ability, one should employ this. This is in line with a statement of University of Amsterdam professor Johan van Benthem, that information is the only resource that increases with use (2000, p. 5). Indeed, the more one uses knowledge, the greater that knowledge becomes, as it is enriched with experience.

We may even take a step further: one of the talents which we as human beings are given, and that characterises us as a species, are our intellectual abilities. We have the intellectual ability to read text on different levels, we have the ability to understand hidden meanings in texts or, if not that, then we have the ability to be critical toward what we are reading because we have been given this faculty. The human ability to understand cannot be neutralised or eliminated, and the existence of a religious text does not give one either the right nor the duty to follow its stipulations slavishly. From the perspective of the Qur'an, this is confirmed in an aya that says that only those who are given understanding will learn (from the Sacred Texts), i.e. Sura Ar Ra'd (13), Aya 20. This indicates that mere text, sacred or not, is not sufficient. Only if it is coupled with understanding (or, in our terminology, with intelligence) it becomes meaningful and imbued with life.

---

[44] It must be said that in Islam, interest is forbidden, which is based on Sura Al Baqarah (2), Aya 277.

The thought that any text, such as the Qur'an, is an ultimate and flawless text, as if history had stopped in the years of its revelation, is arguable. The Qur'an says that, if it were flawed, it would have inconsistencies (see, for example, Sura An Nisa (4), Aya 83), but it is not clear whether it contains such inconsistencies. In one aya, an intoxicating drink made of grapes (probably wine) is understood to be a sign and increase understanding (Sura An Nahl (16), Aya 86), while two other suras (Sura Al Baqarah (2), Aya 220 and Sura Al Maidah (5), Aya 91) prohibit its consumption. According to the Qur'an, sometimes Christians and Jews are believers, sometimes they are not. What these examples seem to indicate is that the Qur'an was conceived in stages. This is most notably perceptible in the suras before and after Mohammad's *hizjra*, his travel from Mecca to Medina in 622.

So then, let us look at a number of examples where we may be able to find hidden meaning in Sacred Texts that may help us look differently at issues in life as well as at these sacred texts themselves.

4

Applications of the theory of two times

Life and death: existence and essence (1)

One of life's greatest mysteries is the hypothesis of its non-existence: death. With this, I do not mean the death of others. The death of others can, at least to an extent, be understood from the perspective of the sciences of perception (i.e. the natural sciences and, in particular, biology). It is simply the absence of life and while there may not exist a clear consensus on a definition of life in the natural sciences, John Dewey's definition of a living being still has considerable merit. According to Dewey (1916/2011) "a living being is one that subjugates and controls for its own continued activity the energies that would otherwise use it up" (pp. 1-2). Once this process terminates, life has ended and death set in. The real mystery is one's own death and what consequences this has for perception, that is to say from the perspective of consciousness: the phenomenology of death. When we understand being as experiencing, as Descartes said, and if death involves the end of experience, then does it entail the end of our existence? This is a question the natural sciences do not have a definitive answer to in as far as they are sciences of (empirical) perceptions, but not of (empirical) perception. If its tenets are valid as long as there are experiences, they do not extend to experience itself and, therefore, cannot explain what happens in its absence.

This is, however, a question that our theory may be able to throw a light on. From our point of view the definition of life, at least human life, is existence in two times. The fact that this encounter inherent in human being includes two innately different dimensions, namely that of the time-defined and that of the timeless, constitutes its paradox: the paradox of life or our existence as what Heinisch called a Mittelwesen (intermediary being). Nevertheless, for many the real paradox of life is that it is, or seems to be, finite. For example according to the existentialist Camus, the finitude of life, reflected by death, makes life inherently absurd (or paradoxical). This induces the notion that the self-evidence of one's existence, i.e. one's consciousness or experience of the here and now, and of perception, is not self-evident at all. How can this be explained? How is one to make sense of that what now so clearly is, as it is perceived, that which is the foundation of everything, every logic, science and value can so definitively disappear? Where conscious perception is the most valued part of the mind, a great perceived discrepancy between life and death can indeed be expected. This may lead to an understandable and probably in part healthy fear of death. An equation that Camus thought could be addressed as follows (1942-1945/2013, p. 197):

Quand tu auras accepté la mort, le problème de Dieu sera résolu
– et non pas l'inverse.

But we don't necessarily agree with Camus, on this occasion and, instead, argue that an understanding of religion can help understand the phenomenon of death. To address the above-mentioned questions, we recall that religion is the locally conditioned response to the mentioned paradox that is inherent in being human, while however recognising that, with that, it did not disappear. In fact, religion itself often appears as paradoxical. Jung observed that religion is paradoxical by nature because only the paradox is partially capable of representing the fullness of life (1970, p. 67). Count Paul Yorck of Wartenburg (quoted by Heidegger, 1927/2006, p. 403) might have had similar thoughts when he said that paradox is a sign of truth.

To be sure, different religions gave different answers to the question of what happens when one dies. In Hinduism and Buddhism, for example, but also among the Druze, there exists a belief in reincarnation. In Hinduism, the concept of Karma is central, which is associated with the individual soul (here Buddhists and a majority of Hinduists part ways, as Buddhists do not necessarily believe the soul is individual). During life, the soul undertakes actions of a moral nature and accordingly accumulates a positive or negative 'sukriti' (akin to a credit for good deeds), which is associated with the soul. With positive sukriti or a good karma, the human being can be elevated in a next life and be reborn with a more auspicious identity. On the other hand, with negative sukriti or karma one can be reincarnated into a person with more challenging circumstances or even an animal. The highest step of this cycle of birth and rebirth, of which the objective is learning, is Brahmaloka or heaven (and in Buddhism, nirvana). Once this afterlife is reached, no further learning is needed and therefore usually no further reincarnation will take place.

In both Christianity and Islam, there also exists an afterlife for which life is understood to be a preparation. In both religions there is a theorem of a Kingdom of Heaven respectively paradise, which is superior to terrestrial life like eternity is superior to the here and now. According to Christianity, the dead will rise again on the Day of Judgement, when those that are righteous will be separated from the others (Revelation 20: 11-15). While the righteous will inherit what one may call the utopia of Christianity, New Jerusalem, others will perish. This idea has been criticised, for example, by the theologians of liberation (a movement originating in South America), who maintained that it reflects an oppressive metaphysical system in that it invites people to suffer oppression during life in the hope that redemption will come after life. This would not induce people to rise up against their conditions of oppression and, therefore, perpetuate injustice in empirical reality, in the here and now. To be clear, our theory explicitly says that we exist in two times, and not only in eternity. Rather than considering that it is right to suffer in the here and now in expectation of eternity, this theory proposes that we will have to import ideals from eternity, such as justice, into the here and now for their application.

Interestingly, a similar criticism on Christianity – albeit with completely different implications – originated in Europe. For Nietzsche, through Christianity, European culture was poisoned from inside: by adhering to an ideal of turning the other cheek, a culture of weakness was instilled; an ethic that would render Western societies unfit to survive in the competition of life, in the Dyonisian fray in which one culture has to assert itself against other cultures for their mere survival. A fray, which, according to Mach (an anthropologist and physicist and one of the predecessors of Einstein's Theory of Relativity[45]) had positive aspects, as:

> ... one would have to be blind not to notice the cultural progress, the competitive, general upswing that has grown from the quarrel between races, even if this struggle in its incidental excesses desperately resembles a striving for humanity via the detour of bestiality (in: Keller 1964, p. 101).

Incidentally, in 'The Genealogy of Moral', Nietzsche described the origins of religion – of Christianity – as a development where the dichotomy good versus bad had evolved into one of good versus evil, whereby a new social function was created: that of the priest, reserved for the weakest members of society. Whereas, first, what was strong was good, according to Nietzsche, these values were inverted in religion. Nietzsche saw a Jewish conspiracy here, writing that:

> It was the Jews who have contested against the aristocratic sense of values (good = distinguished = powerful = beautiful = happy = loved by God) its inversion with a terrifying logic and have held on with the teeth of an abysmal hatred (the hatred of powerlessness) that 'only the misers are the good ones, the poor, the powerless, humble, the suffering, the deprived, sick, hideous are the only pious ones, the only godly, for them alone there will be blessing – on the other hand you, you distinguished and powerful, you will in all eternity be evil' (1887/1968b, p. 281).

Interestingly, as it seems to contradict the above idea, the Qur'an makes the point that Jews like life, at least seemingly with a disapproving undertone, in Sura Al Baqarah (2), Aya 97. But contrarily to the sometimes-evoked image of Islam that it rejects life, the Qur'an not only says

---

[45] Einstein himself once wrote that Mach could have developed the Theory of Relatively himself under different circumstances (1916, p. 103). Popper wrote that, in reality, Mach had rejected the theory as long as he lived (2006, pp. 232-233), but Gereon Wolters (1987) argued that this was a lie diffused by Mach's son Ludwig, who was addicted to cocaine.

that worldly life is but a game and vain pastime (Sura Al An'aam (6), Aya 33) but also indicates that a believer will receive rewards in the present as well as in a next life (Sura Ali Imraan (3), Aya 149). However that may be, a similar thought of Jews as Nietzsche's (albeit seemingly more hostile) had been expressed over 1,500 years earlier, according to St. Augustine (426/2007, p. 308), by Seneca, who argued that:

> The custom of that criminal people has meanwhile spread to the extent that it has entered all countries. The vanquished have given laws to their victors!

It is then no surprise that the idea that Christian culture contributed to the weakness of Europe was picked up as a leading theme of National Socialism. The Nazi culture certainly brought a Dionysian element into European, or more precisely German, politics asserting that Germanic culture was engaged in a struggle on life and death with other cultures, among which the Slavic but, most importantly, Jewish culture and that it was infiltrated by the debilitating ideas of Christianity that were but one instrument to subdue it. Naturally, Nazism was anti-Christian. Further to the ideological justification the Nazis allegedly found in Nietzsche's work, whose concept of the Übermensch was adopted to denote the position of the German race in respect of other races, Primo Levi, in his book 'If This is a Man', in which he described his experiences in Auschwitz, the concentration camp that he survived, wrote that however much Nietzsche's theory may have been fit for misuse, there was one thing that he had not discovered in it: *Schadenfreude*, or the pleasure of the suffering of another human being (2000, p. 528).

It is interesting to see how in Christianity the idea of the importance of life and death merges into a concept of an eternal life and a victory over death. To illustrate: the iconic and probably even constitutive story of the resurrection of the Christ, which is celebrated at the festivity of Easter (in the Northern Hemisphere, near the spring equinox, similarly to how Christmas is located in time near the winter solstice). It is of note that Easter inherited significant fertility-related symbolisms. Of note, because, while these symbolisms probably find their origin in the association of the equinox with new beginnings of life in nature, they are also associated with the permanence of life – with resurrection, possibly not of the individual, but of nature as a whole. Therefore, the resurrection of Jesus, is – unconsciously? – connected with the perpetuation of life. Not individual life, but life itself.

So let us now address the question of death by applying our theory of existence in two times: according to it we simultaneously live in a consciousness, i.e. the world of the here and now, and eternity (the unconscious). What is likely, albeit admittedly speculation, is that we will leave the world of the here and now at some point at the end of our lives and retreat into the 'other world'. But, if this is true, then what will happen to experience with such a transition? Is experience separately from consciousness possible? From the perspective of our theory, consciousness is the manifestation of the temporal dimension of our existence. It is, moreover and as argued earlier, time itself. However, death cannot be an end of eternity as there can, by definition, not be an end to eternity (remarkably, Stein emphasised that eternity is present in life as well as after it, 2009, p. 202). We could expect, as Schopenhauer argued (1818/1996, II, p. 641) that what happens with death is not the end of experience, although it may be the end of one's individuality (1818/1996, I, p. 391), on which conscious perception is based. That is to say, what would disappear with death is 'just' the consciousness of being individual or, in Schopenhauer's own words (1818/1996, I, p. 384):

> Der Tod ist ein Schlaf, in welchem die Individualität vergessen wird: alles andere erwacht wieder oder vielmehr ist wach geblieben.

> Death is a sleep, in which individuality is forgotten: all other things wake up or, rather, have stayed awake.

Interestingly, if this were true, it would make many stories from the Bible and other sacred texts clearer: it would then be more understandable, for example, why existence in the present world – consciousness – is often regarded as a training for the afterlife; why Jesus asked his disciples to leave their worldly lives behind and follow him (Luke 9:

23-24). Yet, in line with our theory that human existence is not only eternity but also takes place in the here and now, rather than asking believers to withdraw from society, sacred texts still often promote action in society: for example, in Christianity all gospels, except that of St. John,[46] say that a camel will rather pass through the eye of a needle than that a rich person will enter into the Kingdom of Heaven (Matthew 19:23-24; Mark 10:24-25; Luke 18:24-25). One may imagine that the rationale for this is that the wealth of one implies perpetuating the poverty of others. This suggests that actions in the present influence our position in the other world; they train us in 'One-ness'. And sometimes, new prophets may help us with this: for example, Schopenhauer said that it is the illusion of existential individuality that signify injustice, evil and cruelty (1818/1996, II, p. 776) and that their appearance in humans are a signal of the strength of that illusion.

Our theory may even help us to arrive at an understanding of the ideas of heaven and hell: for those who have always wanted to separate themselves from others, the realisation that one *is* the other, in the 'other' world, the eternity where our individual identities converge (while the impression, based on consciousness, that one is separate from others is strong), must be a quasi-infernal experience; on the other hand, for who always felt insignificant, excluded and lonely, it must be heavenly to realise that one is in fact 'one' with all the others. To let go of one's consciousness (i.e. life in the here and now), that is, the experiences of the self, of division and separation and dissolve in a sea of others might be heaven for the selfless, for the ones who want to be united with everything, be 'a part of it all'; and in particular for those who are poor, rejected, isolated, oppressed and humble, while it is likely to feel like hell for those that thrive on difference, on being superior to others, arrogant, who believe there is something definitive that divides the 'upper classes' from the 'lower classes' and who are convinced that this life is all there is.

This places the existentialist Sartre's statement (1944/1987), from his play *Huis clos* (translated to 'No exit' in English) that *les autres, c'est l'en-*

---

[46] In general, the gospel of St. John seems to differ in quite many respects from the other three gospels, referred to as the synoptic gospels.

fer (i.e. hell is the others) in a new light. In Huis Clos, main character Garcin finds that dying means that there is no escape from others: no more privacy, no more sleep. Our response to this notion could be that hell can, indeed, be others – but, as mentioned, others could also be heaven. It is then no surprise that, according to Matthew 5:3, the poor in spirit are blessed, as the Kingdom of Heaven is theirs. Or, once again in the words of Schopenhauer (1818/1996, II, p. 649):

> Wir erinnern uns hier, daß der bessere Mensch der ist, welcher zwischen sich und den Anderen den wenigsten Unterschied macht, sie nicht als absolut Nicht-Ich betrachtet, während dem Schlechten dieser Unterscheid groß, ja absolut ist.
>
> We remember here that the better human being is the one who makes between her or himself and others the least difference, does not perceive them as absolute not-I, while this difference is large, even absolute, to the evil one.

Apart from a playwright, Sartre is also known as father of existentialism, the philosophy probably most concerned with the question of death. As is well-known, the existentialists are said to have rejected religion and the idea of a pre-existing metaphysical meaning or essence to life. In a speech of 29 October 1945 in Paris, which was published as *l'Existentialisme est un Humanisme*, Sartre said that the essence of existentialism is that existence precedes essence (1946/1996, p. 26) – in other words, first there is physical human existence and only then, possibly but not necessarily, meaning (essence) can be constructed. While this would seem to imply atheism, the Dutch philosopher Achterhuis, in *De moed om mens te zijn* (The Courage to be Human), dismissed the widely accepted idea that the French existentialist Albert Camus was an atheist (1969, p. 188). While Camus rejected one of the fundamental ideas of Christianity, namely that there is a Kingdom in Heaven for which present life, on earth, is a preparation, Achterhuis argued that Camus would probably have identified with Jewish religion, which, he emphasised, does not have this concept[47] but focuses on life. In the Torah and Old Testament,

---

[47] This point is subject to debate, however, cf. Goldberg and Rayner (1989, pp. 267-269).

even someone who has suffered as much as Job, ultimately received his rewards (wealth, a new family) in life.

Yet another existentialist (Heidegger) gave an early opposite spin to the meaning of death for life: rather than making life absurd, according to Heidegger, Being-towards-death, that is to say the finitude of temporality, is the hidden foundation of the historicity of existence (1927/2006, p. 386). Alternatively formulated, it is but the existence of death, and concern with this, that creates concern or engagement with the world at all (see also pp. 374 & 385). Or, as Heidegger said elsewhere (p. 326): *"Zeitlichkeit enthüllt sich als der Sinn der eigentlichen Sorge"* (temporality reveals itself as the meaning of actual concern). That is to say that only because of death does what happens in life really matter. This suggests that, if there were no death, that is to say, if there were no end to physical essence, there could not be any meaning or essence.

Whether reincarnation exists would be another assessment that is speculative, according to the theory of existence in two worlds, although it would fit well with one of its underpinnings: that 'we', in a sense, are all One in that we coincide with one another in eternity (i.e. that our separation is tenuous and entirely contingent on our condition of consciousness). It would seem to reflect divine justice to have someone, say, a white man, who looks down on persons of other gender and ethnicity, be reborn as a black woman (or, of course, vice versa). As cited by Schopenhauer (1818/1996, II, p. 647), according to Hume, reincarnation ('metempsychosis') is "the only system of this kind that philosophy can hearken to" (p. 1799, 23). However this may be, in summary, religions (almost any religion, not just the so-called monotheistic religions) seem often to say that consciousness is not all there is, that there is an eternity at the bottom of the mind or in any case in a realm beyond conscious perception. This would seem to take away some of the existentialist absurdity of life. In fact, religion almost always conveys the notion that death is not an end. Possibly Schopenhauer knew that when he said (1818/1996, II, p. 741):

> Wenn das Leben an sich selbst ... dem Nichtsein entschieden

vorzuziehn wäre; so brauchte die Ausgangspforte nicht von so entsetzlichen Wächtern, wie der Tod mit seinen Schrecken ist, besetzt zu sein.

If life in itself … would be preferable to non-existence, it would not need to place such fear-instilling guardians at its gates as is the case with death.

A final thought: it is thinkable that the references to an end of time in the New Testament (and later in the movement of Millennialism) are not really references to and end of time, as the collective here and now – that is to say, to an end of the world as we know it – but to a personal end of the here and now, i.e. death. It is then not the end of shared time that we are near to, but, in line with our observation that consciousness is time, near the end of consciousness, which we would commonly understand as death. The encounter of experience with the 'other world' might be one which could be similar to that of which the Book of Revelation speaks. *Memento mori*: life is short and during this life we (also) need to prepare ourselves for the other world, by understanding it – which religious texts, if read correctly, may help us do.

Utopias and ethics: myths of the end (2)

Closely associated with death as an individual destiny is the theme of a collective destiny or end of time. Very often, religions offer a vision of where history is going. As a second example, or case study, let us then examine what some religions believe to occur at the end of collective time. To gain an understanding of this, we should first observe that, in superficial terms, what all religions and, among them, the three monotheistic religions, seem to have in common is that they induce their followers to do what is good. That is to say, they stimulate their adherents to live according to a set of rules devised within the framework of that religion (an ethic), which, within that framework, constitute what is good. These can become laws. In one religion, for example, it can be that good means that one does not kill a cow; in another, it may not be permitted to kill any person; in another yet, it can be that it is considered wrong to kill anyone with the same religion. In South America, the Inca cosmology was governed by the three main tenets *'ama sua, ama llulla, ama quella'*, or: do not steal, do not lie, do not be lazy.

For Kant, what made every human being sacred and an 'end in themselves' is that we have access to an ethical understanding of what is good (*Vernunft* but, this time, in the sense of practical reason, that is to say, reason pertaining not to what is, but to what ought to be done). What makes a human being good, for Kant, is their awareness of the ethical law. In our vocabulary, we could call this access to eternity or, possibly, again, intelligence. For Kant, it would in principle not be allowed to kill anyone, as human beings are all ends in themselves. Now, in order to understand how religions give indications for dealing with one's life world, which includes others not adhering to the same religion or any religion at all, that is to say, an ethic, it must be mentioned that every ethic requires a utopia. This is the reflection of an ideal world, which suggests things that should be done or way that things should be done (an ethic) for the ideal to be established or continued; for example, the utopias of Judaism, Christianity or Islam require an ethic with a view to the realisation of these utopias. This is reminiscent of Kant's notion that (1785/1996, p. 44):

> Die Vorschriften für den Arzt, um seinen Mann auf gründliche Art gesund zu machen, und für einen Giftmischer, um ihn sicher zu töten, sind in sofern von gleichem Wert, als eine jede dazu dient, ihre Absicht vollkommen zu bewirken.

> The procedures for a medical doctor, to rigorously heal a man, and for a poison-mixer, to kill him with certainty, are of the same value to the extent that each of these has the purpose for the objective to be achieved.

This distinction in utopias and ethics seems implied in Kant's identification of practical reason as opposed to pure reason, where the practical represents that, which "through our will can be realised" (1974, p. 242). So, while utopias and ethics are firmly intertwined, any evaluation of an ethic has, as such, to be thoroughly separated from that of its related utopia. While an ethic might be excellent, this excellence is only based on its functionality to achieve the utopia and the utopia it is based on might still be reprehensible from a given moral framework. What is at stake is a question of effectiveness rather than morality, as Berlin said in his famous lecture 'Two Concepts of Liberty':

> Where ends are agreed, the only questions left are those of means, and these are not political but technical, that is to say, capable of being settled by experts or machines like arguments between engineers or doctors (1970, p. 119).

This fact aids an appreciation of why the idea of utopias of religions is rather relevant for understanding their ethics. While, as mentioned earlier, the Christian utopia may be the New Jerusalem; the Jewish one Israel; and the Muslim one the Umma or the re-establishment of the Islamic Empire, there have existed many other utopias throughout history, for example, Plato's Republic; Marx' and Engels' communist society; and More's Utopia (More coined the word utopia, 1516/2001), a forerunner of communist society and heir to Plato's Republic as a place without private property; Fukuyama's liberal democracy, and so on. The Biblical book dealing with the Christian utopia is that of Revelation. This is possibly not coincidentally the most dreamlike and hallucinatory book in the New Testament; a style that fits its nature, in as far as we have identified prophets as intermediaries with the 'other' world or the time of eternity. A further description of the Christian utopia is given in Augustine's City of God, where he contrasted the earthly city of injustice (Rome, in the conventional reading) with the eternal City of God, or New Jerusalem, which is metaphysical. This city unites people regardless of their physical differences:

> So while this heavenly city dwells on earth as a stranger, she calls its citizens from all peoples and gathers its community from among all languages; in this, she does not worry about what may be different among them in terms of customs, their laws or their institutions, aimed at obtaining and maintaining

earthly peace; she does not abolish or cancel any of this; on the contrary, she preserves it and adapts to it, because all that may be different among different people is still aimed at the same thing: earthly peace. The only thing is that it may not become an obstacle for the religion that it is the one and only God that must be honoured. (Augustinus, 426/2007, p. 970)

It is in light of these utopias, including Saint Augustine's, that we can understand the ethics of different religions, such as the Ten Commandments of Moses; their reformulation by Jesus; the Islamic Shar'ia; and the Inca ethic. In all these cases, there can be an understanding of another world, an abstract one, where flawless concepts exist in eternity, but there is in the same time a clear concern with how practical life on earth and in this time is to be organised. The Ten Commandments may seem rudimentary to a modern reader, yet they are still largely aligned with many contemporary ethical systems. Where Jesus is at times perceived to have 'loosened' the law, he emphasised that this impression is wrong; where, in the Old Testament, it is not allowed to commit adultery, for example, with Jesus, even thinking of this is prohibited. Not only the letter of the law is emphasised; so is the thought (spirit) that underpins it. The Shar'ia is again very precise, dealing with practical matters such as nutrition, due process law and how punishment must take place (see Sura An Nisa (4), e.g. Ayas 4, 12-13 and 24-25, and Sura Al Maidah (5), e.g. Ayas 4, 6 and 7).

In line with our earlier idea that Deity has, at times, been thought of as Nature, I argue that these ethical laws tend to refer to what is understood to be a natural order of things, i.e. that they originate in a natural law. As nature represents the way things are, the world of perception, and as inevitably as natural laws predict what will happen, so human beings are subject to a set of laws they will need to follow to adhere to nature, for their own benefit, although they can choose not to obey them. This may well be a leading thought in Plato's Republic: that the righteous minds experience the greatest happiness, because they are aligned with the natural order of things (4th century BCE/1995a, p. 233, 239-240) and the greatest injustice is to do what is not in one's nature. It is, however, in contradiction with Popper's explicit distinction between natural laws and normative laws (1945/2019, p. 55-56). He argued that: "The breakdown of magic tribalism is closely connected with the realization that taboos are different in various tribes, that they are imposed and enforced by man, and that they may be broken without unpleasant repercussions if one can only escape the sanctions imposed by one's fellow men" (p. 58), adding that the standards of normative laws "are not to be found in nature" (p. 59).

So what can we say about this from the perspective of our theory? I argue that conceptions of utopias and ethics, in as far as divine revelation, come from no-time (eternity). However, based on our theory, there are judgements we can make on what are and what are not correct ethics. Let us first take a look at what is possibly the most enduring and pervasive ethical idea in human thought, that of the Golden Rule, which can, in one way or another, be found in most religions and also, interestingly, in what may well be its first explicit formulation, with Chinese sage Confucius (Book XII of the Analects, 3rd century BCE/1979): "Do not impose on others what you yourself do not desire." In Christianity, we find it in Matthew 7:12 and Luke 6:31 and, in Judaism, there is the famous anecdote of the scholar Hillel who is said to have lived in the 1st century BCE and who commented that the essence of the Torah is to not do to others what is hateful to oneself, adding that the rest is its interpretation. As this seems to recognise the essential One-ness of human beings, i.e. that others have the same or similar likes and dislikes as one, it is in line with our theory.

Another application of our theory: one of the main issues that the Golden Rule evokes is the question whether the others that the rule is applicable to, are all others, or only the others of the same group. Here we arrive at Durkheim's theory, presented in 'The Elementary Forms of Religious Life', that the constitution of society coincided with the origin of religion. Durkheim studied the phenomenon of religion through what he considered its most 'primitive' expression, namely Australian indigenous religion. He considered that a group's awareness of this group was constituted under a specific sign, usually an animal, that would become the group's totem (for example, the Kangaroo, making the group the Kangaroo clan). Through this totem, the group was confirmed as a society and, according to Durkheim, this society then became its own Deity as visualised in the totem; further arguing that this defined the difference between the sacred and profane: the sacred is the group; the profane everything else (1912/2008, pp. xix–xxi, Introduction probably by Mark S. Cladis). This raises the question whether the Golden Rule applies to both the sacred and the profane, i.e. to all persons or only the members of the own (national, ethnic or religious) group.

In our theory, however, it is not in society that we find the origin of religion. We have argued that it inheres in the in-born paradox within every human being or every being with 'Vernunft' (reason). And, as we find that we share the depths of our being, i.e. eternity, with other reasonable beings, the sacred – those who are not profane – are all who have this same characteristic, that is to say, all beings with Vernunft, or, in other words, all beings who have this inner paradox, which itself is to say: all people. We could say: *We doubt, therefore we are*. Or even: *We are confused, therefore we are*. Therefore, in summary, Kant rather than Durkheim was right here and the Golden Rule is to apply to all human beings. This is an ethic sanctioned by our theory; however, for now, we can side with Popper in that we do not have to adhere to a specific utopia (even though we might intuit its outlines). We can adhere to an ethic and see where that takes us.

While we side with Popper here, we do not agree with him that the standards of normative laws are not to be found in nature (see above). It contradicts one specifically interesting formulation of the Golden Rule, which lies in the Hindu concept of Karma, mentioned previously, which is essentially understood as a law that says that whatever is given by one, will come back to one. Even so, there are important differences between Hinduism and the Abrahamic religions: in Hinduism, time at macroscopic level is essentially cyclical, going through stages of creation, maintenance and destruction, which are different from individual time, wherein an individual can, effectively, obtain enlightenment. The achievement of enlightenment will lead to an escape from the cycle of rebirth and, as existence in the world is understood to be a punishment, of suffering.

In this worldview, which may seem solipsistic at first sight, history – or time and the events that take place in it – is fundamentally Maya or illusion and in essence serves the growth of the individual, not the development of the world. As mentioned in the previous section, this growth may take place over many rebirths or reincarnations. In this worldview, there is no interest in a collective destiny, or end of time, as the empirical world or, in our vocabulary, the here and now, is not real. This seems similar to Plato's position. Incidentally, in general, the commonalities between several of Plato's views and Hinduism are striking. One may, in particular, mention the existence of three 'castes' in Plato's Republic, which seem similar to those in Hinduism: first there are the philosophers or Brahmans, the 'highest' caste; then the guardians or kṣatrias, which are the second-highest caste; and then there are the citizens. There are also casteless persons. At least as revealing is Saint Augustine's account, in the City of God (426/2007, p. 606), where he attributes a view on afterlife to Plato that seems perfectly inspired by Vedic philosophy:

> Plato meent dus dat de zielen van de stervelingen niet voor altijd in hun lichamen kunnen blijven, maar daaruit door de noodzaak van de dood worden losgemaakt. Hij meent verder, dat ze dan niet voorgoed zonder lichamen blijven voortbestaan, maar dat de mensen zonder ophouden beurtelings van dood levend en van levend weer dood worden, waarbij dan volgens hem het verschil tussen de wijzen en de andere mensen hierin bestaat, dat de wijzen na hun dood naar de sterrenhemel opstijgen en ieder van hen dan op de voor hem geëigende ster een tijd lang rust vindt … . Degenen echter die een onverstandig leven geleid hebben, worden op korte termijn weer in lichamen teruggebracht, mensen- of dierelichamen al naar ze door hun gedrag hebben verdiend.

> Plato thus believes that the souls of mortals cannot stay in their bodies forever but will be free from them through the necessity of their deaths. He further believes that they subsequently do not exist forever without a body but that people incessantly go from death to life and back to death again whereby then, according to him, the difference between the wise and others consists of this, that the wise, after their death rise to the starry sky and each one of them finds rest for a while on a star suited to them. ... However, those that have led an unwise life will be brought back to a body shortly, a human or animal body according to what they deserve based on their behaviour.

In relation to this, and the notion that Plato's work is strongly connected with the original Christian thoughts, it is remarkable that Schopenhauer suggested that Christianity probably has a Hindu origin (1818/1996, II, p. 623), rather than (only) a Jewish one. Schopenhauer, incidentally, greatly admired Hinduism, as manifested when he said (1818/1996, I, p. 487) that:

> In Indien fassen unsere Religionen nie und nimmermehr Wurzel: die Urweisheit des Menschengeschlechts wird nicht von den Begebenheiten in Galiläa verdrängt werden. Hingegen strömt indische Weisheit nach Europa zurück und wird eine Grundveränderung in unserm Wissen und Denken hervorbringen.

> In India our religions will never take hold: the original wisdom of the human race will not be pushed aside by the events in Galilea. On the contrary, Indian wisdom flows back to Europe and will effect a fundamental change in our knowledge and thinking.

Nevertheless, the idea that the present world is not real and is a place that must be sought refuge from, is something that our theory of existence in two worlds does not agree with. Our theory explicitly defines the human condition as confluence of two times, not only one of these. One who lives in consciousness only has no notion of a transcendental truth; but the person who lives in eternity only, is a mystic. While the

Hindu ideal or individual utopia seems to be personified in the mystic, our theory of existence in two times implies we have a responsibility, too, for the world we inhabit in the here and now. We can undertake our actions to fulfil our responsibility, inspired by eternity. In addition, differently from, for example, Judaism, Christianity and Islam, Hinduism is occasionally said to be a polytheistic religion. While the utopias of the monotheistic world religions may be different among one another, this does not necessarily mean there are no ethical similarities. For example, a specific characteristic of the monotheistic religions is, by definition, that they say that there is only one God.

The ethical rule following from this constitutive principle is that it is not allowed to worship any specific thing as a god. This can be explained from what we discussed earlier: if something is a thing it is by definition limited and therefore in contradiction with the characteristics typically ascribed to Deity: i.e. eternal and all-encompassing or omnipresent. On the other hand, what is eternal and all-encompassing can, by this very fact, not be perceived, as what is unlimited does not fit into the intrinsically limited framework of consciousness; which is, among other reasons, why eternity – the other world or time – and consciousness are two strictly divided worlds. Then, what is everything is in the same time nothing, as De Cusa already predicted: nothing or zero is also infinity (1440/1954). For this reason, worship of any thing is, by definition, in contradiction with the foundational principles of monotheism.

Worshiping our Creator then means: worshiping no *thing*, or, in other words, nothing. We are thus not to worship money, ourselves, any ideological movement or ideology or even any other person.[48] We are not even to worship any religion or, speaking of persons, any prophet. The idea that, when we do not worship any thing, the Spirit will come over us, seems to correspond to the idea that we reach the deepest layers in our minds by means of absence. This, however, does not in and by itself mean that our Creator does not have any personal properties. From the perspective of our theory, we hope that the principle behind monothe-

---

[48] Although one might wonder whether the worship of the child Jesus, in Christianity, constitutes a suggestion to, somehow, worship one's children.

ism is understood to be reciprocal: that is to say that, while, as discussed earlier, the ability to view unity in manifoldness helps us recognise one Deity behind all things, this understanding of one Deity itself helps us recognise unity in the manifoldness of the ways in which Deity is recognised, related to and worshiped. That is to say, on the level of utopia, the principle of monotheism may help us realise Deity is not the exclusive property of any manifestation of a people in the here and now. It is not the One Deity of Jewish people, or of the Christians or Muslims. It is one Deity for One people, which are all people; that is to say all human beings that existing in the here and now and with access to eternity (i.e. intelligence), are capable of recognising this Deity.

This suggests our end station is one of Oneness.

Human in exile: the origin, paradise and evil (3)

We have, so far, examined how the human condition as defined in the previous chapter can assist us with a greater understanding of religious stories. In the previous section, in particular, we explored some larger stories of an end station of history, which present a kind utopia that, in turn, provide ethics to guide human behaviour. These stories of the end of times provide us with material to interpret the here and now and events occurring in it. However, while utopias of religion provide the projection of an end of history, the three monotheistic religions (and other religions, such as Shintoism, as well) also have a myth of a beginning, which colour our perceptions of the present (our consciousness). What is their origin? The existence in two times seems to almost automatically create a feeling of exile, as we are banned from eternity. In the monotheistic religions, and Judaism in particular, this feeling has been captured by the myth, or story, of how the human being was chased from paradise. This story seems to be an instance of a phenomenon from evolutionary biology translated to a mythological shape, like with the story of creation.

If this seems rather improbable, it is worth noting a fascinating account related by geologist Salomon Kroonenberg; a story, told in 1865 to a young soldier, by the chief of the Klamath Indians, who live close to Crater Lake in the United States. Crater Lake is located in a crater with a diameter of 12 kilometer, which originated through one of the four greatest volcanic eruptions of the last 10,000 years (2007, p. 121):

> Long ago, when humanity still lived in caves, Llao, the chief of the underworld saw, from the top of the mountain Mazama, a wonderful woman, Loha. He asked her to come with him to the underworld, but she refused. Even the promise that she would become immortal could not convince her. Her people did not want to persuade her to accept Llao's offer. Llao became angry and tried to thunderingly destroy her with fire. Skell, the chief of the upperworld, descended from the skies to the mountain Shasta to come to her [Loha's] aid. In the battle that followed, the sky glowed, and the gods threw burning stones at each other, after that it became dark, the earth shook, fire came from the mountain of Llao and set the trees on fire. The tribe of Loha had to flee to the water of the Klamath Lake. Two brave medicine men, in an attempt to assuage the danger, threw themselves in the glowing mouth of Mazama, Llao's mountain. Skell then made the earth shake so violently that the earth fell on Llao. When finally the dark clouds of ash had descended and light had returned, the mountain had disappeared, and an enormous hole had appeared where the mountain used to be. The curse of the fire had been undone, the hole filled with rainwater and so originated Crater Lake.

Kroonenberg similarly connected ancient stories of natural disasters to events of climatic cyclicity or pulses (catastrophes). For example, when around 9,000 years ago, the last great Ice Age ended, the icecaps of Northern Europe melted, resulting in a significant rise of the sea levels. Kroonenberg speculated that it was this flood that was recorded originally in the Gilgamesh Epos, and which lives on in the Bible, in the story of the Arc of Noah and also in Greek myths; Celtic legends; the Scandinavian Edda; the Bhagavad Gita; and many other legends, stories and myths of peoples worldwide, including in the Americas and Australia

(2007, p. 211).

My contention is that we can use the theory of living in two times here, once again; concomitantly, I believe that the myth of paradise reflects the confluence of two phenomena: first, our present consciousness; and, second, the memory of a pre-human existence when, as a species, from an evolutionary perspective, we were still a part of non-human nature. With being a part of non-human nature I mean that we did not yet have consciousness, did not yet live in time or, with more precision, in the here and now (i.e. we lived only in the time of eternity), did not have a free will and therefore did not have to face the dilemmas created by choice inherent in consciousness – and most of all, the option to do either good or evil, which the Great Inquisitor in Dostoyevsky's parable with the same name so deplored (1879-1880/1958, p. 305 and on).[49] In summary, as a species, we lived in a state that *from the perspective of consciousness*, that is to say, from the view of the here and now, seems very attractive.

There was thus, in reality, never a fall from paradise: there was only an ascent from an animal state to humanity or, differently formulated, from a life only in eternity (the eternity of nature, a cyclical eternity) to one in both times. Eating from the tree of knowledge meant an evolutionary leap forward towards Vernunft – and this Vernunft in pure reason itself implied a submission to an ethical law, in practical reason. This, in turn, is associated with the feelings of shame that befell Adam and Eve after eating from the tree of knowledge. After all, where there is no ethical law, there is also no shame or, rather, there does not need to be any as there is nothing one fell short of. This interpretation seems similar, albeit not entirely equal, to Fromm's in 'The fear of freedom' (1984):

> Man is forbidden to eat from the tree of knowledge of good and evil. He acts against God's command, he breaks through the state of harmony with nature of which he is a part without transcending it. From the standpoint of the Church which rep-

---
[49] See also Tolstoy (1869/2006, p. 495, 499-500).

resented authority, this is essentially sin. From the standpoint of man, however, this is the beginning of human freedom. Acting against God's orders means freeing himself from coercion, emerging from the unconscious existence of prehuman life to the level of man. Acting against the command of authority, committing a sin, is in its positive human aspect the first act of freedom, that is, the first human act. In the myth the sin in its formal aspect is the acting against God's command; in its material aspect it is the eating of the tree of knowledge. The act of disobedience as an act of freedom is the beginning of reason.

Paradise, therefore, consists of these two elements: consciousness, which we beings with reason have by definition (as 'we' includes all who can read this text), and belonging to a greater whole, nature, which we do not, but have a memory of. The illusion which is created by this confluence of things is that there has in the past existed an ideal situation such as paradise. In reality, this is a product of the incapability of the human being to imagine away our consciousness; therefore, when we vaguely remember an existence in harmony with nature, we do so while preserving our consciousness, and thereby (artificially) created a memory of something that never really existed. We now know or at least we can infer from archaeological findings that a paradise never existed in the past. When humanity was still a part of nature, we were subject to it; we were, in other words, not conscious. Nature, to us, was as water to a fish.

However, this notion of paradise has created a certain kind of mimesis within us:[50] the idea of a paradise that, merely because of its conceptual existence (and as laid down in mythology, in the Bible and the Qur'an) humanity will perpetually long for, and that will inspire us in our darkest moments calls for its own realisation. Humanity will attempt to realise it (while we believe we re-establish it), if only because we have this idea, this vague, undefined but still extremely forceful and important notion within us, which is based on our paradoxical existence and the

---

[50] With this I mean the desire to imitate something – in this case, something that never actually existed.

tensions this gives rise to, in ourselves. And this, not coincidentally, seems very similar to the tension in us that makes us look for religion – the search for paradise is a search for meaning that so often finds its expression in a religious exploration. As Schopenhauer (1818/1996, II, p. 208) said:

> Tempel und Kirchen, Pagoden und Moscheen, in allen Landen, aus allen Zeiten, in Pracht und Größe, zeugen vom metaphysischen Bedürfnis des Menschen, welches stark und unvertilgbar dem physischen auf dem Fuße folgt.
>
> Temples and churches, pagodas and mosques, in all countries, from all times, in beauty and size, stand witness to the metaphysical need of the human being, which follows the physical one strongly and ineradicably.

We can, therefore, with a relatively great degree of confidence or faith say that paradise is not in the past but lies in the future, even though to the human being it seems explicitly a memory of times long gone (incidentally, it is an idea we can also find in non-religious texts; for example, Hesiod's Golden Age is located in the past). As such, paradise is, effectively, a memory of the future. Yes: another paradox! And, moreover, a paradox related to time, coined in the last century. A special edition of a Netherlands magazine on utopias was enigmatically called history of the future, but the phrase "hope is a memory of the future" seems to have first appeared in the French philosopher Gabriel Marcel's essay 'Homo viator', where he said (1951, p. 53):

> … if time is in its essence a separation and as it were a perpetual splitting up of the self in relation to itself, hope on the contrary aims at reunion, at recollection, at reconciliation: in that way, and in that way alone, it might be called a memory of the future.

In this context, it is important to quote Heidegger (1927/2006), who emphasised the importance of the existence of a future for understanding oneself when he said (p. 336) that:

> Zukunft ermöglicht ontologisch ein Seiendes, das so ist, daß es verstehend in seinem Sein-können existiert.
>
> Future ontologically enables an existence (being) that is such that it can exist in its being with understanding.

While, contrary to utopia, paradise does not seem to be a social or collective ideal, paradise, and in particular the yearning for it, may well be at the heart of all utopias: they often reflect an end station of history that represents in the same time an origin that has always been there, i.e. is located in eternity and a place we return to (e.g. Marx' communist society), a natural order that is restored and the outcome of an inevitable, natural process. As a consequence, the laws that these utopias prescribe – that is to say, their ethics – are assumed to be moral laws, but firmly founded in nature, that is human nature, and therefore referring to a way things are. But we can learn even more from the myth of Paradise. There may be a consensus that, in symbolic terms, the 'fall' from Eden marks the end of an innocence of the human species, as theological thought tends to interpret this as the introduction of evil through the disruption of a natural order in which we are thought to have lived. From the perspective of our theory, we can observe that, if that is indeed the case, then the introduction of evil takes place at the same time as the birth of consciousness (i.e. time) and, for that reason, with the birth of humankind as such.

This suggests that thinking and evil are contingent upon one another. And indeed, as to the question of evil in creation, it seems one can say that, without suffering, there could never have been thinking. Evil, or rather suffering as a consequence of evil (in strict rigour, one might say that without suffering there is no evil) is the inevitable and necessary pre-condition for thinking. The reason for this is that thinking is fundamentally rooted in the basic question 'why?' This question (why?) would or could never be posed if all were good. It is unlikely that the animal asks: why? In that sense, we can say that suffering (or evil) is the source of philosophy, evil understood as the fragmented state of the human condition, different from original unity, and as a result of the human faculty of choice (which itself is a consequence of consciousness). Thus, the end of paradise gave human beings the two tools needed to think: knowledge or cognition and, in the fundamentally divided world – or two worlds – in which we live, freedom through choice, philosophically translated to evil.[51] This suggests that growth, without at least some 'evil', might not be possible. After all, as Schopenhauer said (1818/1996, II, p. 208):

> Wenn unser Leben endlos und schmerzlos wäre, würde es vielleicht doch keinem einfallen zu fragen, warum die Welt da sei und gerade diese Beschaffenheit habe; sondern eben auch sich alles von selbst verstehn.

> If our lives were infinite and painless, it would probably occur to no-one to ask why the world exists and is exactly the way it is; everything would be understandable by itself.

Or, even more clearly (1818/1996, II, p. 222):

Die soeben ausgesprochene nähere Beschaffenheit des Erstaunens, welches zum Philosophieren treibt, entspringt offenbar aus dem Anblick *des Übels und des Bösen* in der Welt ... .

The characteristics of astonishment expressed just now, which led to the act of philosophy, apparently originate in the experience of evil in the world.

This analysis itself might help us reinterpret another religious story: that of Job in the Old Testament. Many theologians consider this as one of the most difficult stories of the Bible, in that it deals with the question of the manifestation of evil in relation to the omnipotence of God (a question traditionally dealt with in a theodicy). Not only theologians have tried their hand at this story, philosophers have also done so, for example the Dutch philosopher Awee Prins in his work on *ennui* (the feeling of meaninglessness that he diagnoses as symptomatic of West-

---

[51] This seems akin to the question whether we should abandon the knife because one can, potentially, do evil with it.

ern culture) in which he says: "when existence is reduced to a completely intolerable state, powers are unleashed that make real life possible" (2007, p. 28). This might be a correct view from the perspective of our theory and we might add: while evil certainly is not intelligent, only it can effect intelligence.

Therefore, just like the intellectual or prophet unites local circumstances with concepts from beyond to define rules (an ethic) for life, applied to specific times and places, so it might be the task of every person to attempt to realise the paradise or the ideal we envision to reach at the end of history (say, world peace) on earth. Saint Augustine defended the *Civitate Dei* of New Jerusalem against the city of the world. What we might have to do now is bring this city 'down to earth'. Naturally, as soon as pure concepts reach this earth, like angels, they stain themselves with the soil that cannot be found in heaven. But this does not mean that these concepts will vanquish. It could mean that they will grow into something from the soil or will be used to build something with – the mud from the Lagoon of Venice, which Magris described in *Microcosmi* is, in the same time, dirty and the warm and humid substance from which all life originates (1998, pp. 56-58).

Time and the other: stories of creation (4)

But we can go even further back in time and ask how religions see creation, i.e. how they explain the existence of anything at all. The Abrahamic religions have similar myths of creation, although the Islamic one differs somewhat from the Judaic and the Christian one, whereas, according to Shintoism and ancient Greek religion, in the beginning, there was chaos. Hindus, on the other hand, believe in continuous creation, destruction and regeneration on a macroscopic scale. In Hinduism, we relatively recently (around 5,000 years ago), entered the Era of Kali (Kali Yuga), a time of destruction. We are witness to the cosmic order falling apart and, while this happens, it is our individual challenge to detach ourselves from the destruction of the universe. A detachment from beauty: Isidore of Seville said, in Book VIII of his Etymologies (in

Eco, 2010, p. 82), that the Greek word 'kosmos' means ornament, due to the beauty of nature.

In whichever way myths of creation differ across religions, they coincide in one, crucial point: they always denote a beginning of time (which is true even for the Big Bang) or, rather, non-eternity. That is, of course, fundamental for our theory of existence in two times. It is from the moment of creation that time split in two: while the time of eternity has continued to exist, creation meant the beginning of the time of consciousness. That is to say that the essence of the human condition started with the moment of creation, even though the human species did not yet exist. And while creation stories, such as the myth of creation in Genesis may appear like evidence that religion did not have a correct grasp of science, they can, occasionally, also be considered surprisingly accurate accounts of how the cosmos was created first; then the planet; animals; and finally human beings, as mentioned earlier. From the perspective of our theory, what we can learn from this and similar stories is the fundamental importance of time, its interwovenness with the very fabric of our existence through how it co-determines our consciousness.

At this point, it may be helpful to recall how Freud thought of religion as a response to helplessness in the face of nature. A helplessness reduced through the natural sciences; sciences that have at least two languages to discuss nature: biology, which offered evolution theory against the myth of creation; and physics, which has monopolised thought about time. From the perspective of our theory, the validity of these sciences does not imply that the creation myths are void; we just re-interpret them: myths of creation suggest they reflect when time started; our theory suggests they reflect when consciousness started. They describe an encounter between time and non-time; between culture and nature. Humanity, which in part originates in the conceptual world that underpins perception, which we attribute our essence to, meets nature through consciousness – an encounter that almost automatically implies the finitude of bodily life. Nature, for humanity, has to be the great 'Other'; that which it meets in the here and now, as its direct substance of conscious perception, but does not coincide with, at least not entirely. This has a paradoxical element to it, because, in the same time, human originates from Nature.

It is then probably no coincidence that the expression 'the Other', meant to emphasise the difference from one self, comes from the field of cultural anthropology, a particular discipline that some consider anachronistic and possibly inherently discriminatory. The reason for this is that cultural anthropology studies other cultures, assuming the existence of a central culture (the Western one) that provides a framework from which other, non-Western cultures can be studied. In other words, the Western world takes on the role of classifier while the rest of the world is classified. It may be the suggestion that other cultures can be a subject (or, depending on terminology, object of study rather than subjects in their own right), and thus subjected to study, that troubles the anthropologist. Cultures are under scrutiny or, at least, that is what their subjugation to study implies. In this regard, cultural anthropology is similar to psychoanalysis, where the human mind is subjected to study – objectivised – and therefore not anymore only that what studies. What is considered uncomfortable about this is that, in cultural anthropology, human is conceived as a part of Nature, as a natural phenomenon that can be captured in a taxonomy. How could this happen?

In 'The Order of Things', Foucault compellingly argued that the human sciences came into existence in the 19th century as a result of a process of secularisation through which the existing sciences, such as natural history, were infiltrated by the factor of time (1966/2005). While the world as it existed previously was assumed to have been created and then stayed unchanged, scientific discoveries, or their interpretation, began to suggest that the world as we know it had not always been the same: accumulative evidence from archaeology and geology indicated that the face of the earth, with its rivers, valleys, deserts and mountains, seas and glaciers had not at one point in time been created and remained unchanged from then on, but had evolved through quantities of time that far surpassed what even until the 17th century had been believed to be the age of the earth (Savorgnan di Brazza, 1941, p. 81), that is to say, not more than 6,000 years old (see e.g. Saint Augustine, 426/2007, p. 555). This itself was an idea that could cause that, as Kroonenberg wrote, Archbishop James Ussher calculated in the year 1654 that the creation of the earth had taken place on 22 October 4004 BCE (2007, p. 48).

Biology, as a science, did therefore not yet exist in Ussher's time and in its place, there was natural history. According to Foucault, this could not yet be a science of life, as biology is, simply because life as a concept did not exist prior to the 19th century. Natural history was the science of phenomena of nature rather than the study of nature, and life, as a developing entity. Something similar was the case with linguistics: that was the study of the diffusion of languages after Babel, after the Biblical story of the dispersal of people following the fall of the Tower of Babel. This means there was a hypothesis of an original language that had been spoken prior to the fall, of which each existing language was thought to still preserve a kernel. For some linguists, the challenge lay in discovering, in each language, their aspect of the original language. Foucault said that this changed with Darwin's theory of evolution. It was not the case that no-one before Darwin had thought of the possibility that nature developed, but no-one had, so far, hypothesised that it developed completely independently of a plan, without predefined outcome, that is in an open time. Epistemologically, this seems similar to the juxtaposition of utopia (closed time), that is to say history with a pre-defined outcome, with the open society of Popper (open time).

According to Foucault, evolution theory changed, more than anything else, the perception of time. And with that, Foucault argued, it changed everything: it showed that time was a factor in creating reality as we know it, a reality that is fluid. This development brought an as of yet undiscovered actor to the forefront of the stage: the human being. Foucault noted that we had never been an object of study before. He also noted that, with the theory of evolution, this human being was thrown into a state of existential uncertainty of which Nietzsche may have been the most articulate spokesperson. We could say that, in 1859, we ate from the tree of knowledge once again and, possibly not coincidentally, not much later, Nietzsche proclaimed the death of our Creator (e.g. in 1885/1968a, p. 290). Incidentally, the historian of science Debora Meijer observed that, from that point in time, museums started to classify their works in a different way than had hitherto been the case. Whereas art exhibitions had previously been ordered by artist or thematically, in accordance with the idea that time did not really exist or that it was not essential to the order of things, from then on, works were beginning to be ordered chronologically. From then on, we started to have the notion of 'eras' or 'periods'. (Prior to then, one can say, there existed only one classical, timeless ideal, which one could either be closer to or further away from.)

Instead of a closed time, such as that of Christianity, in which there is a beginning described by the book of Genesis, a clear caesura (the age of mercy that started with Jesus) and the announcement of an end (the Day of Judgement and, finally, the New Jerusalem), Darwin had unlocked a universe with a fundamentally open horizon. It is no coincidence that the dispute between some theists and atheists is waged to this day largely around the subject of evolution. Among some theists, there exists the idea that what appears to be evolution is, in fact, intelligent design. On this issue, Darwin would have disagreed; he had written, in a letter of 1861 to John Frederick William Herschel (1994, p. 135):

> One cannot look at this Universe with all living productions & man without believing that all has been intelligently designed; yet when I look to each individual organism, I can see no evidence of this.

What is important and significant in this development for our theory of existence in two times, which equates consciousness with time, is that the 'discovery of time' resulted in the appearance of the human being on the stage of the theatre of academic study, which marked the origin of the social and human sciences. As Kwa stated (1992, p. 220), before this time, the human being was one of the species to be classified in accordance with the divine order of the Book of Nature. From then on, it became clear or rather, it was thought that there is no divine order.

Therefore, the human being emerged as the classifying species. As it became clear that the scientist was not unveiling nature as it existentially is, but ordering it, according to an order that is, itself, inherently human, the question emerged: what is a human order? And: what is a human being?

This question resulted in the birth of two sciences in particular: psychoanalysis, of Freud; and cultural anthropology by Boas, Malinowski and Mach. It is interesting, said Foucault, that these sciences are characterised by a nature rediscovered in and about human beings, that is, however, construed as Other: in cultural anthropology, other peoples (or cultures) and, with more precision, the Primitive; in psychoanalysis, unconsciousness that, as Freud noted, is connected with the great themes of mythology and art and, to understand and interpret it, knowledge of general culture is indispensable (1991, p. 188). Both these encounters with the Other are also encounters with Nature. Only this time, the encounters are with nature in humanity. Nietzsche is cited by Foucault as one discoverer of the unconscious and forerunner of introspective psychology when he asked 'who speaks when I speak?' (2005). The dichotomy he applied to art, itself the human interpretation of nature (or nature replicated through the lens of humanity) as Apollonian or Dionysian is a conceptualisation of nature. In the Apollonian perspective, nature is like an English garden: neat, ordered and cultivated; in the Dionysian one, it is untamed wilderness, intoxicating and unifying (for the 16th and 17th century English philosopher Francis Bacon a garden represented the purest of pleasures (1597/1985, p. 197) and, therefore, a piece of heaven on earth; so the designation of paradise as a Garden of Eden seems well-chosen[52]).

In the concept of the Barbarian, the Other (the other human being) is identified as part of the same species, but as a part of nature rather than of civilisation and, moreover, as Dionysian. The human sciences are the first possibility in history to speak with nature, because through ('primitive') human beings, nature had acquired a voice and, as a conse-

---

[52] The word paradise itself probably originates from the Persian word pairidaeza, which means secluded garden (Manuel & Manuel, 1982, p. 38).

quence, there was a possibility to speak with what is beyond it – nature – and transcends it. That is to say, there is a possibility to speak with the other time, with eternity (and, as discussed earlier, to this effect cultural anthropology and psychoanalysis developed instruments to interrogate the Other: in psychoanalysis, mainly, the interview, in cultural anthropology, mainly, observation). While the possibility of this conversation with the other time in one self is still the rational ground of our theory of existence in two times, and while the idea that people from other cultures are more 'primitive' – and from another time – has, fortunately, lost legitimacy since, in parts of the 19th and 20th century this held sway.

The anthropologist Johannes Fabian specifically noted how time had historically been used – instrumentalised – to distinguish between peoples; indeed, how time was constructed as a political instrument to relegate peoples different from Europeans to a realm of primitivity that helped justify their subjugation for the sake of spreading civilisation (1983, p. 17). To this end, different kinds of time were developed with the help of anthropology: "Anthropology contributed above all to the intellectual justification of the colonial enterprise. It gave to politics and economics […] a firm belief in 'natural' i.e. evolutionary Time". Fabian argued that time is, in essence, a human construct, used to develop a human reality. By dividing the world in territories – we here, the other there - in fact using these territories to define one self, Fabian said, Western culture developed the concept of temporal territories, where other cultures are said to inhabit other periods of time, possibly one that 'our culture' had already been through.

Therefore in some older *schemata*, primitive people were depicted as lagging behind in time, on the basis of the assumption that there exists one linear movement or route of human development. This implied that there was also only one possible end station, to which Europeans were thought to be closer than others. This idea that Europe was the continent with the most modern culture and that the further peoples lived away from it, the more primitive they are and, as a consequence, the more they were 'behind', was captured in a diagram by Fabian (1983, p. 27):

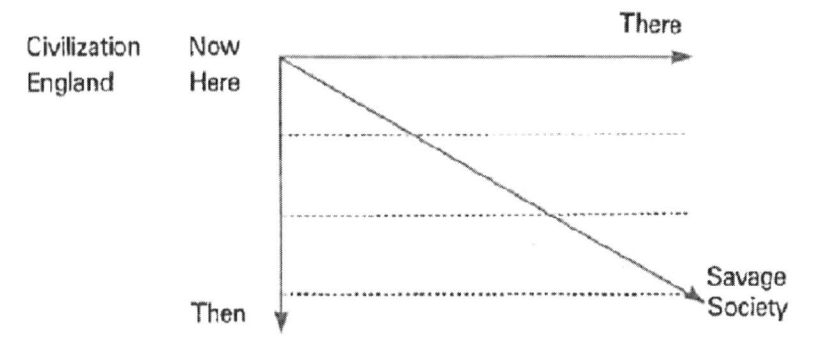

Figure 2 *Fabian's interpretation of the renaissance mind-set on civilisation & time.*

The British philosopher Stephen Toulmin argued that however well-intentioned Descartes' mission mentioned earlier might have been, it was also a precursor to the view of history as a unique timeline and, as a consequence, the notion that Europeans had progressed more along this line than others (1990). After all Descartes' objective was to devise a system based on mathematical truths that would be equally true for all, regardless of religion. Here, Magris might have perceived the universalistic force of modernism that, however positive in some respects, would also swallow up the special, particular and local (a force similar to the one we now call globalisation) against which the Habsburg Dynasty sought to protect the world by preserving tradition. The universalistic model, in any case, allowed for the development of a universal timeline of civilisation (see e.g. Van der Loo and Van Reijen 1990, p. 18), which, of course, its inventors could own. Counter-voices, Toulmin said, existed from the beginning, for example in the persons of Giambattista Vico and Johann Herder, who argued that the value of a culture cannot be understood except from the perspective of that culture itself and that there is an inherent value in these different perspectives.

While Darwin's theory of evolution has been misused to suggest some cultures were more evolved more than others, there exists another, newer epistemological model of time that makes this difficult: Einstein's theory of (special) relativity. Its basic idea is, at least in part, retractable to the human sciences (as mentioned earlier, some of its preparatory work was undertaken by the Moravian physicist and cultural anthropologist Mach), and it is not unreasonable to assume that the system called cultural relativism reflects a translation of this framework back into the human sciences. After all, nowadays, the notion that cultures are equivalent and that their value can only be understood from their own perspective, that is, they are relative to themselves, is widely accepted in social theory (e.g. De Swaan in: Ramdas 1993, p. 13). From a philosophical perspective, a main contribution from this theory is that, when there are several frameworks from which to measure a movement of objects (say, the trajectory of a stone thrown either from a train window or from along the track), there is not one superior framework. In Newtonian physics, by contrast, there existed a (hypothetical) privileged framework. The re-translation of this (scientific) idea to cultural anthropology was that no cultural framework should be considered superior to others. Frameworks exist vis-à-vis each other, but none should be taken as the privileged one.

In this respect it may be of interest to note that Gerald Holton identified 'thematic' similarities between Mach and Einstein (1973, introduction): both of them, for example, were anti-racist. To illustrate the relevance of this parallel between a political and a scientific position, bridged by general epistemology, Katherine Arens (1989, p. 218) wrote that "Mach assumes that the knowledge each people possesses will only be informative relative to the desires and values of their culture's frame of references." It is indeed likely that a theory with the specific implication of the theory of special relativity had to be developed by someone who would endorse the epistemological implications this would have. And with relevance to our theory in two times, we see here reflected the idea that, in principle, each consciousness (i.e. time-space position, or place) is equivalent; and the principles of eternity can be translated to each place.

The above is yet another example that conceptions regarding the foundations of reality, say, metaphysical conceptions (sometimes erroneously considered 'only' physical), are somehow value-neutral. Politics, political principles and political environments engender specific scientific or philosophical theories and vice versa: to this effect. I mentioned the examples of how Toulmin explained the development of Descartes' theory and how Marx thought he could derive the ideal social order on a scientific basis; we can add numerous other examples of the relation between the social and the scientific, for example, that a Hindu conception of circular time may influence action in physical reality. For this reason, it remains important to follow Popper's example in continuing to think across the dividing lines of the philosophy of science and political philosophy.

The gendered body: encounter of spirit, angel and animal (5)

The discovery of humanity in the sciences is of importance within the framework of this exploration, as we observed that truth, including religious truth, is contingent on the set-up of the mind or the human condition in general. However, the birth of the conscious mind coincided with something that the mind is conscious of, including, at some point, the material mind and, therefore, the body. In the conventional natural sciences the body is also the carrier of that mind. And even though we might think that reality is arranged 'idealistically', the body still anchors us in the here and now – crucial to our existence in two times – and it establishes our main relationship with nature. Or, as Schopenhauer, said, while (the perception of) space might exist only in my head, empirically, my head is located in space (1818/1996, II, p. 31).

There has always a problematic element in that relation: (biological) nature has never been an exclusively positive concept, as it represented the opposite of spirit and eternity, the seductions of the flesh and the potential of decay; things that human beings preferred to not identify with. In the Catholic Church, and not only that institution, nature has traditionally been that what had to be overcome: nature was the part of the human being – the body – that would induce him or her to engage in sin, engage with the temporal and sensual pleasures that have the potential to corrupt the soul, itself rooted in eternity. As the Kingdom of Heaven and the City of God were thought of as metaphysical territories – existing beyond time and space – they had to be distinguished from the clay of the earth. While, according to the Bible, human beings were created as man and woman (i.e. as bodies), sin and lust were traditionally viewed as connected to the body and its senses. Inclined as the body is to sin, the Church recommended people to focus on the Spirit instead. The very fact that Catholic clergy, or a Hindu sanyasi, cannot marry, is rooted in this idea: without a wife, without sex and engagement in physical pleasure, without the confrontation with the cycle of life (children) and the engagement with the mundane tasks this entails, the priest would be more able to focus on religious values and fulfil his (usually his) role.[53]

Of the two main ideas connected to the body, that women – say, human beings with a female body – are inferior and that men should refrain from desiring women if they intended to be spiritual leaders, only the first is mentioned explicitly in main sacred texts. For example, in the Bhagavad Gita all main actors are men (Krishna and Arjuna) as are main (demi-) gods, such as Shiva, Brahman and Ganesha. Although a few are female (Saraswati, Lakhsmi), they tend to be the consorts of male deities. In fact, it is noteworthy that the main female goddess Kali, the consort of Shiva, is considered a goddess of time, i.e. the time of change. In Judaism, and while there are a few female protagonists such as Esther and Judith, the main prophets are male, notably Moses. Judaic laws of purity forbid vicinity of women during menstruation (Leviticus 15:19-33). Similar pictures emerge in Christianity and Islam, where the main spiritual leaders tend(ed) to be men and even in some aboriginal Australian practices, women were not allowed access to certain sacred places (Durkheim, 1912/2008).

In several cases, the distinctions that are made between women and men tend to cross into territories that would not be in line with understandings of equality as laid out in a normative contemporary text such as the Universal Declaration of Human Rights (UDHR). In the Qur'an, there is

---

[53] Needless to say, because of this vision, women themselves could never become part of the clergy.

an indication that the testimony of one man is equivalent to that of two women, i.e. Al Baaqarah (2), Aya 283. Moreover, the Qur'an says that men, in general, stand above women.[54] The Bible also includes several passages that state the superiority of men over women, both in the Old and the New Testament (e.g. 1 Timothy 2:11-14, 1 Corinthians 14:34-35, Ephesians 5:22 and Colossians 3:18). This idea is usually explained as having to be seen in a context where the man is a breadwinner, a position that lays a specific burden on him and which, through this burden, provided him with a chance of development. It is this burden and his development, Nahed Selim (2003, p. 95) argued, that increased the value of his testimony, not the mere fact of being a man. The implication of this, she added, is that this inequality is not due to gender *per se*, but to a set of circumstances where sex relates to a specific task distribution. Does this constellation change, then it would seem reasonable for the difference in the value of testimonies to change equally.

What has become practice, that male spiritual leaders and notably the Catholic clergy and Hindu sanyasins refrain from marriage, may be rooted in, but is not directly mandated by sacred texts. The justification for this is related to the previously mentioned idea, to say it in the language of our theory of existence in two worlds, that activities in the here and now – and the body, which represents the here and now *par excellence*, is the carrier of one of these times – distract from engagement with the other time. According to Francis Bacon, a person – in his time, probably, a man – could either have a family with children, raise them and in this way contribute to the world, or be alone, and dedicate himself to the advancement of the sciences, and in that way contribute to the world (1597/1985, p. 81). Similarly, but earlier, Saint Augustine (426/2007, p. 1112) quoted Paul, in 1 Corinthians 7:5 saying that who does not have a wife, thinks about divine things and how to please God.

While this sounds logical from the perspective of our theory, the relatively recently revealed scandals of child abuse in the Catholic Church suggest that something is not quite right here. This hearkens back to our thesis that the human condition is explicitly not made up of either

---

[54] In Sura An Nisa (4), Aya 35.

our existence in the here and now or eternity, but of both. It suggests that, for a spiritual leader, only life in the time of eternity is insufficient. Rather, it is the encounter with life as it is, the cycle of life and engagement in physical pleasure as well as the duties of running a family, that is, being a man or a woman rather than just a human being, that enriches and informs metaphysical thought just like sciences do not only exist in theoretical concepts, but need nature to apply these concepts to, as much as vice versa.

One example that contradicts the stereotype that genius is inevitably associated with loneliness, suffering and alienation (or even insanity, as addressed earlier) is that of possibly the most celebrated composer in history, Johann Sebastian Bach. Bach allegedly led a happy family life, with many children of which several have become celebrated composers in their own right. Supposedly his only 'transgression' consisted in a coffee addiction. In a different context, the Italian author Claudio Magris spoke of loneliness as a 'false predictor of profundity' (2001a). It is the balance between the spirit and the body, culture and nature, that is to say, the existence in two times that one would expect a religious person to embody. Or, as the Roman poet Juvenal said in his 'Satires': *mens sana in corpore sano*. The prohibition of marriage for clergy seems to inhibit this. One would not ask for marital advice – which can come in valuable at times – from someone who has the role of wise person in a community, but no experience whatsoever in this field.

It seems Islam seeks civilisation in limiting what is supposed to be human's natural state (i.e. repression) at least as strongly as Christianity, which is clearest in its efforts to stamp out any reference to sexuality in the public realm. The tension between worldly pleasures and spiritual development is reflected in Islam in the concept of the 'great' jihad: traditionally, this is the battle against evil within, such as the wish to commit adultery and the presupposition is that this is what humanity is naturally inclined to do. It holds that, earlier, humanity lived in the period of the *jaziliya*, a period of ignorance leading to evil actions. In most Muslim countries, many women wear a *hijab* (headscarf), although in others, such as Turkey, they used not to be allowed in public buildings (this recently changed). The rationale behind the rule for women to cover their shoulders would seem to be that a man is naturally inclined to be distracted by the attractiveness of women and the solution to eliminate such attractiveness from the public realm. The justification for this comes from the Qur'an, which requests women to cover themselves up to their shoulders (Sura An Nour (24), Aya 32). It has become a contested symbol after France forbade wearing it in public places including schools. This fits within the French philosophy of *laïcité*, the division between Church and State, which relegates religion to the private realm. In an unexpected declaration, the high Mufti of Al Azhar in Egypt, likely the highest Sunni Muslim authority in existence, endorsed this move as this concerned 'their', i.e. the predominantly Christian, French territory.

With relevance to Christianity, in his best-seller 'The Da Vinci Code' US author Dan Brown posited that the witch hunts that pestered Europe in the Middle Ages were caused by a female challenge to the authority of the Church. As women, with their bodies, rather than the Church, were considered the holders of the keys to the 'gates to heaven', their potential for power was recognised as enormous (one may, for example, think of Aristophanes' comedy Lysistrata, in which Greek wives forced their husbands to end a war by abstaining from sex, 411 BCE/1970, p. 85). They possessed what we can now, with thanks to Catherine Hakim (2010) label 'erotic capital' and, for that reason, were seen as a threat to the authority of the Church in a way not dissimilar to the threat of the scientific revolution. Needless to say, the idea that attractiveness of women is a source of power relates not only to the rule of celibacy for the clergy, or to that of wearing the hijab in Islam, but also, and more in general, to the notion that mind (ratio) stands above matter (the body). In Paradise, a myth that appears in Judaism, Christianity and Islam, on the other hand, Adam and Eve did not wear clothes. It is the separation from nature that made human beings feel shame and cover ourselves.

In these scenarios, the woman as the 'embodiment of the body', seems to appear as a force of nature and, more precisely, a Dionysian force, which upsets the neat Apollonian order of men. Man had reserved for himself the higher position of access to deeper layers of truth (as expressed in Jung's archetype of the wise old man, 1970, p. 44), whereas the woman posited herself as voice of nature (see, for example, Saint Augustine, 426/2007, p. 1163), the cycle of life, as an advocate, as it were, of matter,[55] and who, in the view of some men, tempt them with the enjoyments of the here and now, as a mystery of irresistibility and powerlessness, as Horkheimer and Adorno expressed it (1944/2007, p. 85), and therefore as a paradox of a combination of weakness and strength, but which interrupts his flights in the heavens of intellectual understanding. In the Middle Ages in particular, the body was, as Le Goff said, viewed as lower than the mind, which might have seemed to support the notion of danger associated with women.

While Freudian ideas around gender – that the Father represents the law, while the Mother represents love and that patriarchy was a victory of the intellect over the physical, as it required "a step forward in culture, since maternity is proved by the senses whereas paternity is an inference based on a deduction and a premise" (1939/1967, pp. 145-146) – may look benign, they seem to say, in essence, something similar: that women are, by nature, through their bodies, more connected with the physical world than men. For Schopenhauer, life perpetuates itself at the cost of people, or rather life is ready to sacrifice the individual at any time (1818/1996, p. 382). In his view, will represents the body and the focal point of this will is the act of procreation (1818/1996, II, p. 730) or sexuality. This is where the full force of will becomes visible. Schopenhauer also argued that women may have significant talent, but not genius, because they will always remain subjective (1818/1996, II, p. 506). Nevertheless, recent empirical data from the world of educational statistics speak of a worldwide trend of female learners performing at least at the same levels as male ones, if not higher.[56] This suggests that, given a chance, women will produce as many geniuses as men, for example, persons such as the great thinker Maria Montessori.

---

[55] The Qur'an compares women to a field in Sura Al Baqarah (2), Aya 224; in Greek mythology, the goddess Gaia represents the earth.

[56] In 'The future of an illusion', Freud (1927/1962) wrote that the idea that women suffer "from a lesser intelligence than men" is "disputable" (p. 61).

What can we say about this from the point of view of our theory, understanding what should be perfectly obvious, i.e. the equivalence of women and men? We can and should say that it is the human and not only the male condition to live in two times. In addition, even if it were true that, due to their bodily condition – including hormones – women would be more tied to the 'here and now' than men are, it must be repeated that it is not one's existence in eternity that results in a connection with Vernunft or being human – it explicitly is our co-existence in two times. In the words of Edith Stein (2009, p. 335): "The body is ... what the soul needs to mediate all its activity beyond the body", that is to say to act in the world, adding that the "living human body is as it were the scene in which and around which the life of the soul unfolds as well as the tool that extends its effectiveness beyond itself" (id., p. 351). The body is also what the soul needs to learn as, in Hinduism, it is the gateway to Maya, the world of illusion. In this view, the soul and body may be disconnected, but the body gives the soul an opportunity to learn exactly because it invites a wide range of mistakes, supposedly in a range of bodies, through reincarnation. To illustrate, this wonderful story:

> A man once asked Deity: what is Maya? The Deity is responded: I will tell you, but first go and fetch me a bucket of water at the well. The man went and, at the well, encountered an extremely beautiful woman. He spoke with her and, as he fell in love, forgot about the request of the Deity and went on his way with her. They settled down, had children and became prosperous. However, one day, the dams of the adjacent river broke and destroyed the man's house and killed his wife and children. The man lost his consciousness and woke up beside the Deity. The Deity then said to him: this is Maya.

War and identity (6)

Can our theory of existence in two times also help us understand the way in which religions, through their narratives of identity, relate to other groups? With relevance to this, among its many other aspects, religion is human connection to a greater, cosmological whole. Whereas the primary function of religions may not directly be to unite humanity, the existence of other peoples, with possibly other religions, is a fact which religious texts do engage with. The Qur'an, in this regard, emphasises that there is a lesson in the diversity of humankind (Sura Ar Rum (30), Aya 23). However, the Qur'an is also the story of the birth of Islam and its assertion vis-à-vis Judaism, Christianity and other religious groups of the 7th century (the Qur'an specifically mentions the Sabians); the Torah or Old Testament is not just a religious book in the traditional sense of the word, but also the ancient story of the Jewish people and, as Horkheimer and Adorno said, just "like the great Asian systems, pre-Christian Judaism was a faith that was hardly separated from national life, from generic self-preservation" (1944/2007, p. 193). The Christian Bible is also the story of the secession of a group of Jews who founded a new religion and became Christians.

In religions as large stories in this sense, their purpose seems to be and have been to create and sustain an identity through shared beliefs. As mentioned earlier, it seems to be a naïve perception that religions such as Judaism, Christianity, Islam or Hinduism have by definition sought peace or to 'unite humanity' except, possibly, under their own banner. While disagreeing with his hypothesis of the origin of religion, pragmatically, some elements of Durkheim's theory presented in 'The elementary forms of religious life' seem true: that religion circles around the group, and that its main function of distinguishing between what is sacred and what profane is, in reality, a demarcation between the (sacred) group and others (the profane, 1912/2008). Moreover, the concept of peace itself has at times been problematised, for example, in the context of the Israeli occupation of Palestinian lands in the sense that if there is no violence (negative peace), but no justice either, then the Norwegian founder of peace studies John Galtung (1964) would say that there is no positive peace. Peace (negative peace) is not only the ultimate idyllic destination of humanity but also the status quo of the ruler (see e.g. Gur Ze'ev, 2000).

In Judaism in particular, the functions of religion and culture seem to largely coincide: the assimilation of Jews into non-Jewish societies has, albeit controversially, been referred to as a 'silent Holocaust'.[57] Hajo G. Meyer, theoretical physicist by education and leader of the Dutch movement Another Jewish Voice, identified two conceptions of Judaism in the Torah: one, universalistic and humanistic, promoted by most prophets; and one nationalistic, promoted for example by Joshua (2007, pp. 2-3). In a similar way, Islam has been referred to as Arabic nationalism (Naipaul, 1991, pp. 4-7). In addition to the great Jihad, in Islam, there is also the concept of the lesser Jihad, which refers to the outward struggle for justice, which may include armed struggle. The Qur'an does not lack in descriptions of how 'unbelievers' (i.e. non-Muslims[58]) should be fought and this lesser Jihad is hardly smaller than the great Jihad but is, rather, its reflection in the 'real' world or, in the language of our theory, the here and now. Like the intention of the great Jihad is to fight evil in one self, on the scale of the microcosm, the intention of the lesser Jihad is to fight evil in the macrocosm. And, in Islam, evil is to a great extent or even entirely, equal to unbelief.

One can say that Islam for itself embodies the 'last idea' in a Hegelian sense: it sees itself as a utopia or description of an ultimate world order. However, unlike liberal democracy in Fukuyama's vision, it does not envision that it will realise world dominance only by its power of conviction, but that it may have to be realised through conquest as well. Islam, which itself is an idea, or at least emanates from the world of ideas, has, as it were, to be transferred into the here and now and so to be materialised. This naturally entails a political order and, in the Sh'ia branch of Islam, the division between religion and state is often considered artificial. In that sense, for many Muslims, the Islamic Empire or universal community of Muslims (*'Umma*) is the embodiment of a Kingdom of Heaven on earth. The 'Umma already exists in the bond of Muslims, worldwide, between one another. It is a trans-national entity in expectation of the final triumph of Islam over its enemies.

---

[57] This term was used, for example, by the American rabbi Ephraim Buchwald.
[58] Given some passages in the Qur'an, particularly in the suras Al Maidah and At Tawbah, it seems hardly tenable to exclude Christians and Jews from this group.

The utopia of Islam lies also, in a sense, in the past, as its rule was once realised in the great Arabic Empire (the preferred name for which is the Islamic Empire, stressing the link between nation and religion), which, at the height of its power, stretched from Central Asia to Andalusia in Spain. The idea that has occasionally been promoted that this was an enlightened nation has to be put into context: one of who are now known as the greatest men of science of the Arab world, Averroes (*Ibn Rushd*) from Spain, had his books burnt publicly on the order of the Khalif. The reason for this: he professed that the truths of religion (revelation) and science (reason) are not necessarily contradictory (cf. Goodman and Russell, 1991). This was considered profane, as revelation was considered superior to reason (see earlier discussion).

The objective of the lesser Jihad is to bring the revelations of Mohammad to the entire world. The issue one might encounter in this is that believing that these revelations are valuable as revelations (and, therefore, not as under scrutiny of reasoned examination) is an act of faith, and not everyone may be prepared to accept this idea. That is not to say that there is no common ground between Islam and Christianity (and possibly Judaism and other religions). However, violence as sanctioned in the lesser Jihad could become an oppressive way of imposing a truth and the idea of a common ground presupposes that there is an encounter of two or more cultures that can learn from one another, and therefore teach each other lessons rather than assuming that one of these cultures is the owner of an unstained, definitive truth, while the other one is inferior.

Of course, Islam is far from alone in that some forces opt for forcible imposition of its ideas and, ultimately, its utopia. In his book '*De hel dat is de ander*' (Hell is the Other, a title seemingly inspired by Sartre), Dutch documentary-maker Bart Brandsma explored the common ground between Muslims and Christians, rather than between Islam and Christianity. This brings him to Jerusalem, among other places, where he spoke with Jewish scholar Yeshayahu Leibowitz, who said that a decision can never be an act of knowledge but is always an act of will (2006, p. 82), where being capable of a will distinguishes human beings from other creatures.⁵⁹ This view seems in no small part inspired by Schopenhauer and reveals an important tension, which we touched upon before: all human beings are defined by the fact that we live both in the here and now and in a time of eternity; we discussed that this eternity defines, after a process of translation as undertaken by the prophets of each era, different rules for each time or 'now'. However, it seems fair to say that the same is the case for each 'here', or place, and thus for each culture inhabiting a certain place. While this does open a way for universalism (with which I mean here the fundamental equivalence of all cultures), it does not need to lead to complete ethical relativism, as the equivalence of cultures as a whole does not imply equivalence of each element constituting an ethical rule in a given culture.

It may be of interest to reiterate here that, while we saw similarities in the ethics of different religions, often encoded as allegories or smaller stories within texts, we also saw differences in utopias, or larger stories, which define the identity of a religious group that, for example, in Judaism largely coincides with the identity of an ethnic group. What Leibovitz seems to have said is that, if utopias collide, decisions have to be made that are not acts of knowledge but of will. The difference between utopias and knowledge is that the latter, but not the former, can, at least in principle, be shared across religious or cultural groups. In some cases, a settlement with persons from other cultural and religious backgrounds can only be established by force: one person or group believes one thing, another believes something else and then, in some cases, the strongest one decides. Or rather, who is the strongest is right: here we recognise, of course, the right of the strongest or 'law of the jungle' (according to Popper, 1945/2019, formulated by the Greek poet Pindar)

It seems that the principle described in Footnote 19 can be applied to the philosophy of Leibowitz: it seems to be conditioned by his political circumstances and consciously or unconsciously justifies a political agenda that might be his country's. The situation in Israel is such that a main

---

⁵⁹ The identification of man with his will), can also be found in Nietzsche's work 'Also sprach Zarathustra' (1885/1968a).

justification some Israeli Jews believe they find in occupying land that historically belonged to (Arab) Palestinians, is the notion that this land (Israel) was given to the Jewish people by God (presumably, in addition to their history there). If there is still any doubt left on the intention of some Zionist Jews to expel Palestinians from their lands at least from the early 20th century, one is referred to Asher Ginzburg's essay 'Truth from Palestine' (Ginzburg is also known as Ahad Ha'am), e.g. in Cohn-Sherbok (2007, p. 10), Ali (2003, p. 90) and Avineri (1981, p. 123). However, Ginzburg himself thought Israel should be a Jewish State where the Arab inhabitants could benefit from the same spiritual values that Judaism possesses, rather than a State for Jews, which would exclude non-Jews, and thus Arabs (in: Cohn-Sherbok, 2007, pp. 8-9; Ha'am, 1962, p. 78-79).

If the idea is that there exists a super-natural law stipulating that the land of Israel is intrinsically the property of the Jewish people, then the question arises: how can this be accepted without rational justification? How would this differ from accepting the words of the Prophet Mohammad at face value? Without justification, such beliefs non-examined by reason can be a ground for conflict and, from the perspective of our theory, the idea that a specific land is destined for a specific ethnos is a problematic one or, rather, we find nothing in it that would support it. Above, we discussed that true faith implies worshiping no 'thing' and that would include a piece of land. We also said that a mission inherent in our theory is that we should bring ideas from 'heaven' to 'earth'. So, if a State would be a place, or framework, to bring an idea from eternity to earth, from the perspective of our theory that would be positive. However, if the idea is to exclude persons based on their ethnicity, then that seems to reflect the perpetuation of Durkheim's idea and not in line with our theory – and therefore negative.

Leibowitz likely knew that his is a truth Israeli Jews cannot share with Christian and Muslim Palestinians. He possibly meant to say that even this truth is not an act of knowledge, but an act of will. That is to say, to believe that the land of Israel is given to and belongs to Jews, is a decision on the basis of a desire. Indeed, the land of Israel / Palestine is certainly one of the most fertile parts of the Near East, which often consists of vast stretches of desert. It is known that the Northwestern Near East or Levant (or what is known as the Mashreq or Greater Syria, *bilad i sham*) has not always been Arabic. It was populated by Syriac and Phoenician, and occasionally Christian, populations, until the 6th and 7th centuries' Arab invasions when Islamic conquerors spread their religion throughout the region. However this may be, Leibovitz' philosophy is not neutral. It seems rooted in the inevitable realisation that his idea is reasonably untenable and that, therefore, violence may be necessary to maintain a status quo. This is not the view of all Jewish people or even of all Jewish Israelis. Groups such as some orthodox haredim and hasedim do not agree Israel is or should be the utopia of Judaism prior to the return of the Messiah (not to mention groups such as 'A Jewish Voice for Peace', based in the United States).

Further to our idea that time may be going backward, mentioned earlier, we can say that any real justification of attributing the land of Israel to the Jewish people can only lie in the future: that is, Israel must provide the facilities of a state to its population, whatever they are (legal, security, utilities, social justice and so on). This is what justifies, for example, the American enterprise if the original population, now have a better chance of a good life than they would have had if European history had ignored the Americas (although the suffering the Native Americans endured at the hand of the occupiers should in no way be marginalised). It is likely, however, that the original Palestinians, largely refugees in the surrounding countries of Lebanon, Syria and Jordan do not see their situation this way. From our point of view, the problem with Leibovitz and his likes is that they seem not able to imagine being others. The important test, from the perspective of our theory of two times, which Leibovitz' philosophy (and nationalist conceptions of religion in general) does not pass is the following: if we accept the idea that all persons belong to two times, a here and now and an eternity, but only temporarily to the here and now and eternally to eternity, would we support the same position if we were in another 'here and now', that is to say, if we were someone else?

While Leibowitz' philosophy is conditioned by what is perceived as a political imperative similarly to Descartes', in their implications, they are diametrically opposed: whereas the mission of Descartes is to prepare a universalistic foundation to achieve peace, Leibowitz suggested that this universalism is not attainable. He drew the final consequence from his ideas, saying to his interviewer Brandsma that, in case of diverging wills, he either would have to kill Brandsma or vice versa (2006, p. 83). Brandsma described how they subsequently laughed, but one is left with the intuition that it is unease and not the comical value of the remark that caused the laughter. We could say that, if at any stage a religion crystallises, it becomes rooted in axiomatic positions of which the truth values can only be imposed, not convince. It entrenches itself against other religions and the emphasis is on difference: this is when religion becomes, once again, nationalism in disguise. This is not to say, of course, that will is in any way inherently negative. Will is also (positive) engagement and, with Stein, we agree that, for human beings willing is quite naturally integrated in our way of understanding when she suggested (2009, pp. 176-177) that:

> Between the person's taking in the world through his understanding and shaping the world through his willing lies an inner give-and-take with the world in his emotions or sense appetite [*Gemüt*]. As a rule, the spiritual subject does not merely encounter an object in the understanding; it does more than receive it in knowledge. The subject is inwardly affected by the object and challenged to take a stance on it.

Adding (later on in her book) that a "will act is the decision to set out for a goal" (id., p. 347). We do not say that we prefer a detachment from will as we might see it in Buddhism, for example; after all, we believe in existence in two times, including the here and now; but we do say that our will is something we should examine.

While Islam prides itself on valuing all human races equally, and indeed the Qur'an says to this effect that human beings have been created differently so that they may know one another (Sura Hoed (11), Aya 119 and Sura Ar Roem (30), Aya 23), it does not recognise the religions of these other peoples as equal. It does not condemn other ethnicities or races, but other cultures and habits may be considered equivalent to the jaziliya as replaced with Islam. In addition, it tends to be emphasised that the Qur'an was revealed in Arabic, suggesting a privileged place for the Arab culture in Islam. In addition, the profession of faith (shahada) is one of the pillars of Islam (in addition to charity (zakat); prayer (salah); pilgrimage (hajj); and fasting (suwm), while Jihad is not) and, in mainstream Islam, one cannot be a Muslim without the profession of faith. The shahada, for its part, not only states that there is only one God, which to most monotheistic believers is true (*la Allah ill'Allah*), but also that Mohammad is His Prophet (*Mohammad el rasool* – more accurately, a *rasool* is a messenger). This constitutes a problem to most Jews and Christians, who do not recognise Mohammad as a Prophet, let alone mention only his name in the profession of faith.

Christianity seems, in this respect, different from both Judaism and Islam, as there is no real connection between religion (*ethos*) and people (*ethnos*). Europeans are not privilegedly Christian, although admittedly the leader of the Catholic Church, or Pope, was European until very recently and even the current, South American pope is of European descent. Its founders, Saint Paul and Jesus, were not Europeans themselves. In the view of the German-Jewish theologian Franz Rosenzweig, this is in line with Christianity's function. According to him (Cohn-Sherbok, 2007, p. 178):

> Judaism ... constitutes the basic relationship between God, humanity and the world. Christianity, on the other hand, has the unique function of including all nations in the revealed relationship with the Divine.

While Judaism is strongly connected with the Jewish people (in fact it integrates the people with its values, history and culture, rather than perceiving them as different elements), Christianity is, in principle, universalistic. In that sense, one might say it is Platonist: not only does it identify a unity behind the manifoldness of sensory perception, it also sees a unity in humanity, where each of its members has access to that unity and can, therefore, in principle, be a Christian. Saint Augustine in

Civitate Dei (The City of God) emphasised that Plato's ideas themselves are, from a Christian point of view, not necessarily wrong (426/2007, pp. 106-107). In fact, the relations between Platonism and Christianity may go even further than Saint Augustine suggested: one can compare the passage in Symposium about love (4th century BCE/1995b, p. 33) with Paul's 1st letter to the Corinthians (1–13), which is also about love. The similarities are striking.

There seems to be something quite particular about this universalistic nature of Christianity: this, and the ethic of turning the other cheek, is at times connected with a rhetoric of an Old Europe, which is tired (see earlier discussion); one which relates the presumably Christian idea of universalism to a typical European decadence, which spells decay and is a precursor to the disappearance of Europe on the international scene as a significant political, cultural and economic presence[60] – a decay that may be seen against the background of an ascent of economies such as China, India and Brazil and steeped in a symbology referring to Empires of the past, notably the Roman one. Some of the most significant Christian leaders of the last century, such as Martin Luther King (American) or Desmond Tutu (South African), were not European either. King, incidentally, is a good example of the previously mentioned prophet, as he proffered a vision of another reality, for example, in his speech of 28 August 1963 at the Lincoln Memorial in Washington DC: 'I have a dream'. This dream, of racial equality came true, at least formally in some places of the world and, in this sense, King saw the future.

In this context, it is of interest to recall the initial history of Christianity: it was, originally, a sect within Judaism and there do not seem to be indications that it was Jesus' intention to separate Christianity from it. However, Saint Paul distanced himself from traditional Judaism when he wrote, in his Letter to the Romans (2: 14), that: "Indeed, when Gen-

---

[60] Although it would be blatantly incorrect to narrow down the multifaceted identity of Europe to only one of its contributory sources, Christianity, leaving out all the others, among which Greek philosophy, mythology and theatre, Roman law, medieval manufacture and guild systems, alchemy, arts and sciences of the Renaissance, the Enlightenment, the French Revolution and its ideals, the Industrial Revolution, German romanticism, and so on.

tiles, who do not have the law, do by nature things required by the law, they are a law for themselves, even though they do not have the law". With this statement, in Christianity, the bond between ethnos and religion was broken. From the perspective of our theory of existence in two times, it cannot be supposed that one ethnos is more closely associated with the other time than any of the other ones. This, of course, contradicts the idea that there exist a chosen people, an ethnos that is closer to Deity than others. It seems rather more reasonable to accept that, like physical characteristics of human beings respond to their specific environment, different religions correspond with local solutions to the very constitutive paradox of human existence in two times.

In recognising this identity – or unity – in the multiplicity of peoples, and their constitutive histories lies, according to Schopenhauer (1818/1996, II, p. 570), the main task of philosophy of history in general:

> ... sie soll also das Identische in allen Vorgängen der alten wie der neuen Zeit, des Orients wie des Okzidents erkennen und trotz aller Verschiedenheit der speziellen Umstände, des Kostümes und der Sitten überall die selbe Menschheit erblicken. ... Die Devise der Geschichte überhaupt müßte lauten: »Eadem, sed aliter« (dasselbe, aber auf andere Weise).

> ... it should therefore recognise the identical in all events of ancient as well as new times, of the east as well as of the west and in spite of all differences in specific circumstances, of costumes and of customs see everywhere the same humanity. ... The motto of history in general should be: »Eadem, sed aliter« (the same, but differently).

This seems reminiscent of Nicolas De Cusa's position (1440/1954, p. 37) that "there is but one essence of all things, which in a diversity of ways is shared." In primal religions or what has been referred to as animism, the idea of unity of all things even has a central position (and I remind the reader that Durkheim developed his theory of religion from 'observations' of Australian 'primitive' religion, 1912/2008), as the following story of a native American person who had entered university suggests

(Smith 1958/1991):

> Oren Lyons was the first Onondagan to enter college. When he returned to his reservation for his first vacation, his uncle proposed a fishing trip on a lake. Once he had his nephew in the middle of the lake where he wanted him, he began to interrogate him. "Well, Oren," he said, "you've been to college; you must be pretty smart now from all they've been teaching you. Let me ask you a question. Who are you?" Taken aback by the question, Oren fumbled for an answer. "What do you mean, who am I? Why, I'm your nephew, of course." His uncle rejected his answer and repeated his question. Successively, the nephew ventured that he was Oren Lyons, an Onondagan, a human being, a man, a young man, all to no avail. When his uncle had reduced him to silence and he asked to be informed as to who he was, his uncle said, "Do you see that bluff over there? Oren, you are that bluff. And that giant pine on the other shore? Oren, you are that pine. And this water that supports our boat? You are this water."

In a column in the International Herald Tribune, the American opinion leader Roger Cohen (2007) reported on an American evangelist who believed that the Jews are the chosen people. This 'fact' would save the Jews in Israel by divine intervention, if necessary, in the conflict with the Palestinians. This thought of the Jewish people as chosen seems widespread among Christians in the United States, often themselves Zionists[61] and the question of Jewish chosennes has been addressed on many occasions, for example by Popper (1945/2019), Freud (1927/1961) and Spinoza (1862). I wrote to Cohen, at the time, that, before the Second World War, the Japanese believed to be a chosen people, saved from two successive Mongolian invasions by a *kamikaze* (divine wind). This contributed to the belief that Japan would be led to a victory by higher powers in its war against America. We now know that Japan was not successful in that war. To speak with Claudio Magris, we probably

---

[61] Zionism is the political movement that supports the return of the Jewish people to their historical homeland in Israel.

have to learn that history makes the loser of yesterday into the winner of tomorrow (2001a, pp. 229-230). It is our association with truth, whatever it is, rather than anything else that makes us powerful. And this truth might lie in that chosen people are all those who live in two times, that is to say: all human beings.

It would nevertheless be false not to remember, at this point, Saint Augustine's words that believing in possessing divine origins increases one's boldness (426/2007, p. 138):

> According to him [Varro] it is useful for states if their strong men think that they descend from gods, even if that is not true. Because for this reason, the human spirit, trusting on its presumed divine origin, would commence with less fear on great enterprises, take on these enterprises with greater energy and so, exactly because of this greater feeling of certainty, complete these with more success.

The magical power of beliefs…

Animals and food (7)

The relationship with animals, except as food, is one which the monotheistic religions seem to provide limited views on. In Hinduism, where the cow is regarded a holy animal, this might be somewhat different due to the concept of reincarnation in that religion but, in general, animals seem to have a more important place in totemic religions. Even so, the Italian Saint Francis of Assisi is said to have been able to communicate with birds; Noah, on his Ark, saved all animal species from a great flood and, in Paradise, Adam and Eve lived in harmony with all animals – except, of course, the snake. This silence of religion stands in contrast to views in philosophy, where a range of opinions is represented: from Descartes' idea that animals are devoid of feeling to Pythagoras' denunciation of the crime of eating meat, a pleasure that he regarded as having a high and bloody cost. There is also the Italian philosopher Giorgio Agamben's comment on the appearance of the eschatological animals in the miniatures of a 13th century Hebrew Bible in the Ambrosiana of Milan that, he argued, reflected the reconciliation of human beings with their animal nature at the end of time (p. 13). Still, according to Agamben, the humanisation of animals implies the animalisation of the human being (2003, p. 86).

So then, the myth of Paradise notwithstanding, and in spite of Isaias 11:6 according to which "the lion shall lie down with the lamb", possibly the main references to animals in the Bible and the Qur'an relate to food laws: the Bible forbids Jews to eat any marine creatures without scales, for example, while the Qur'an forbids Muslims to eat pork meat (why many Hindus are vegetarian seems to be less straightforward). The Christian absence of such strict food laws is usually attributed to the verse of Mark 7:15, which says that it is behaviour rather than what a human being ingests that makes her or him unclean. The treatment of animals has for some time now been under public scrutiny in the context of what is called the 'bio-industry': the industry that provides society with meat for consumption. This has met with controversy during epidemics such as foot and mouth disease (FMD) and mad cow disease (BSE). In reaction to perceived large-scale animal abuse, Netherlands professor Paul Cliteur argued that animals should be granted full 'animal rights' (2001).[62]

Former Food and Agricultural Organisation (FAO) high-level official Louise Fresco believed that food should be part of the canon of daily life but is, in fact, often a blind spot: many prefer not to know or be reminded of where their food comes from, rather than from a shop or market. This is wrong, Fresco said, as one is what one eats, also in the political sense (2007, p. 4). But it seems that food refers to too great an extent to a physical aspect of being human for comfort. Food seems to disrupt Apollonian depictions of nature that seem prevalent, in favour of a Dionysian one, of eating and being eaten. Food (meat more so than vegetables), seems to perpetuate the impression of an unethical nature, of an aspect of ourselves that is in discord with the image of a life in

---

[62] There is one animation film on Internet which links the alleged wrongs of the bio-industry to popular culture, accusing it of creating images that have nothing to do with actual reality: the Meatrix, so named after the movie 'The Matrix', which can be retrieved from http://www.themeatrix.com.

harmony with nature as portrayed in the ideal of Paradise and that of the ecological movement.

It is interesting to speculate what role the emergence of evolution theory has played in the issue at hand. Certainly, it made the line between animal and human being thinner, even more arbitrary, and raised the question to what extent eating meat is engaging in a form of cannibalism.[63] The delicacy of this relation seems to lie in a question that Giorgio Agamben addressed: that of 'snobism' or civilisation. As Kojève said (in Agamben, 2003, p. 18), 'no animal can be a snob'. Here, snobism is the extent to which humanity transcends its (physical) nature. Kojève believed that the Japanese people, with their ritual suicide, were particular snobs. He saw the American lifestyle with its emphasis on comfort, on the other hand, as animalistic. Related to this notion of snobism is the consequence of seeing human beings as civilised animals, i.e. Kwa's 'classifying species' of after the diffusion of evolution theory. The unease resulting from this seems best expressed in the critique of anthropology. Are other ethnic groups 'lower' in the hierarchy of living things, closer to the animal, less snobistic? There is the shame of Europeans having associated people of colour (but some English associated some Irish) with apes, with more primitive species. How sensitive this is, in the context of religion, is illustrated by the outrage over the 2001 Al Moumni affair, in which a Muslim cleric in the Netherlands called Westerners 'lower than dogs and pigs' or the qualification of Jews as 'offspring of apes and pigs'.

Such comparisons can also be found in Sacred Texts. Jesus, a Jew, is said to have once said that one should not take the bread from the children and throw it to the dogs (Mark 7:27), meaning non-Jews. Richard Dawkins cited the Jewish scholar Maimonides in discussing murder, indicating that it is not allowed under Jewish law if a Jewish person is

---

[63] In the Netherlands, an Animal Party was established in 2002 (even though animals can neither be party members nor are part of the electorate), of which the founder was associated with the Seventh-day Adventist Church. Curiously, a Netherlands writer and party member named Maarten 't Hart denounced her in a national newspaper, saying that her leadership of the party is in conflict with her religious affiliation.

murdered. But: "Needless to say, one is not put to death if he kills a heathen" (2007, p. 289). This raises the question to what extent a heathen is seen as a human being at all. The Qur'an strictly forbids killing another believer, while the omission to prohibit killing any human being is suggestive. This once more suggests the relevance of Durkheim's idea that religion is what denotes the difference between the sacred and the profane: i.e. one's group is sacred and the others are profane (1912/2008), which, as mentioned earlier, is different from our position.

According to the principle we have developed, based, in one way or another, on Kant's conception of Vernunft, i.e. that the human condition is defined by its living in two worlds, and its sacredness based on its participation in eternity while still being conscious, which defines our essential paradoxicality along with our freedom, which is not the case for animals, from the perspective of our theory, we have to ultimately draw a sharp line between human beings and animals. As Stein (2009, p. 261) said: "What distinguishes the human soul from the animal soul is the fact that the human soul is *spiritual*". Therefore, the murder of anyone who participates in the here and now, whatever their religion may be, must be strictly prohibited. Even so, there are no indications in our theory that support cruelty against animals and we have to be particularly careful with 'higher' animals that seem to have some level of Vernunft.

5

Final reflections

The land of two times

In the above seven case studies we have taken a brief look at a number of important issues addressed in different world religions and at the extent to which our theory could aid in the interpretation of sacred texts in understanding these issues. In doing so, we sought to reconcile reason with revelation by subjecting original texts to new readings, in pursuit of something that I would, tentatively, call truth. This is not that unconventional: several sacred texts identify Deity with truth; for example, the Qur'an says this in Sura Al Hajj (22), Aya 63. In so far, s/he who seeks truth, seeks Deity. I will close this work with three final reflections. The first (this one) focuses on the political implications of this theory and, in particular, the existence of the other time. I will argue that, if there are any, they suggest the importance of an open society akin to Popper's definition of this. The second reflection will address the extent to which there exists an intuition of the other world in the arts. Finally, I will discuss how we might understand ourselves as human beings, and our role in a greater scheme of things, from the perspective of the proposed theory.

If and when addressing the political implications of this theory, and probably of any theory in the field of religion, a first reaction might be one of rejection; that there should be none. If so, we would follow Dostoyevsky's interpretation of this question for Christianity. He argued that the point at which the Church united itself with worldly power is the moment when it strayed from its Christian principles ('The Grand Inquisitor', 1879-1880/1958). During his stay in the desert, Jesus refused the temptations of Satan, including the promise of power over all nations (worldly power). To Dostoyevsky, the refusal of worldly power is crucial for the mission of the Church so as not to corrupt its spiritual values. When the Church accepted to become the state religion of the Roman Empire, under the patronage of Emperor Theodosius II and Gratian,[64] it accepted the temptation of power and so, in Dostoyevsky's view, opened itself to being corrupted; a corruption that found its zenith in the Spanish Inquisition. This is the historical context in which this story of the Grand Inquisitor is set. However, one could argue that the association of a Church and a state is not that far-fetched, in principle, if religion and ethics are thought of as connected.

After all, the connection between laws and ethics is not controversial (although one realises that what is legal is not always ethical) and it is relatively widely accepted that, in general, the state is the source of the law (see, for example, Bos, 1996, pp. 9 -10), or formalised ethics, of which the practical imperative is grounded in the understanding that a law cannot exist without a mechanism that allows for its enforcement. The Church itself is often considered a community: *extra ecclesia nulla salus* (outside the church, there is no salvation). This idea implies that the human being has to live in a community to be one self. Aloneness is neither the ethic or the utopia (end station) of Christianity or most other religions. This notion itself corresponds with the structuralist idea that the group makes the individual, as much as individuals shape the group. That is to say, a group gives individuals an identity, or a point of reference; it gives him or her a frame for conceiving themselves as someone, to know oneself in the encounter and confrontation with others.

This implies that we find God also in a community, rather than (only) in the desert or another place where we are not disturbed by anyone, and where we can dive deeply into ourselves – far away from the marketplace that Nietzsche's Zarathustra despised, as he sought contact with animals rather than human beings (1885/1968a, p. 62). We can see Deity in the contact with other persons, in the faces of others: there do we find the forgiveness, mercy, compassion, encouragement and affection that every human being longs for. Or, as Dutch 'atheist priest' Hendrikse (2006) wrote:

---

[64] The following separation of the Empire in an Eastern and Western half led to the schism of the Church into the Orthodox and Catholic ones.

Therefore it is better not to say that God exists, but that God happens. Or, more carefully: can happen. Because something only happens if one goes on his way. ... And if God happens, this does not happen without people. Chiefly: if it is not about people, it can not be about God. Also in the Bible, it is never about God-on-His-own. ... If people do what the Bible says about God (be reliable, loving, righteous), they realise what 'I will be there' means. ... To be more precise is almost impossible: if you look for God, you have to go to the people.

The connection between state and religion has been explained differently in different times and places: in the case of Judaism, some Orthodox Jews have traditionally been firmly opposed to the existence of Israel as the embodiment of a Jewish State. In their view, Israel may only be established once the Jewish Messiah has come which, many believe, is not yet the case. For now, according to Orthodox Jews, Judaism must be a spiritual and not a legal-political entity. Christianity is a state religion in several countries, while the Seat of the Catholic Church is an independent country, the Vatican (or Holy See). In France, on the other hand, the concept of *laicité* has involved a strict separation between the state and church (or organised religion, cf. earlier discussion). Iran established an Islamic Republic in 1979, with a government form that has been referred to as 'theocracy'.

Ethics – as in morality – and politics (with which I mean: power) are forces that are at times considered to oppose one another, in religion. It occasionally seems that ethics create stronger communities than politics do. While communities of shared values may seem to be more durable than those created by force, all three Abrahamic religions have gone through a transformation from a community of ethics to a political community. In Islam, this shift seems to have occurred first with the hizjra (the move from Mecca to Medina) of the Prophet Mohammad and has continued with the establishment and expansion of the Islamic Empire; in Christianity, it occurred with the moment the Church decided to assume worldly power (as described by Dostoyevsky) rather than with the mission of St. Paul, who intended to create a community of values rather than a political entity; and in the case of Judaism, quite obviously with the State of Israel.

I argue that, to interpret the implications of these shifts, it is helpful to refer to St. Augustine's reflections in De Civitate Dei. In this key work, St. Augustine described the City of God, which is understood to be (New) Jerusalem, and the city of the earth, which is either Rome or Babel (Babylon), but often believed to be Rome. Augustine explicitly emphasised the metaphysical nature of these cities. That is to say, the earthly Jerusalem is not the City of God, and the real Rome not the New Babylon.[65] The Civitate Dei was imagined as a purely metaphysical entity and, therefore, the division between the mentioned cities is, to an extent, equal to that between empirical reality and metaphysics: the Civitate Dei represents the idea that there is a metaphysical dimension (our 'time of eternity') that precedes physical reality and will, ultimately, like Hegel's *Weltgeist*, assert itself on earth in physical reality (the here and now). It is itself a metaphor.

Any confusion between these realms – broadly the here and now and eternity – materialises faith and therefore facilitates a degeneration into superstition. As discussed previously, religion, or most religions, expressly forbid worshiping anything. This does not preclude that the idea enshrined in the Civitate Dei could assert itself in Jerusalem, but not rather there than anywhere else. Or, otherwise said, New Jerusalem can be anywhere. In summary, the Civitate Dei is a city or community of values, like the 'Umma. It is a spiritual community, where people congregate, guided by meaning. In this sense, we could identify it with the 'real Church' that C.S. Lewis referred to in 'The Screwtape Letters' (1961, p. 13). But if we accept this conception, then does this mean that there are no political implications of our theory? Must we agree with

---

[65] The campaign just prior to the American invasion in Iraq (location of the ancient Babylon) in 2002, in which a section of public opinion was mobilised, seems reminiscent of Cato's repetitive call to destroy the then greatest opponent of Rome, Carthage. Cato ended any of his speeches in the Senate with the formula 'and by the way, I think we should destroy Carthage' (in: Pleticha & Schönberger, 1980, p. 22): *ceterum censeo Carthaginem esse delendam*, possibly one of the first recorded examples of propaganda. Saint Augustine observed that having itself liberated of its greatest fear had not brought Rome peace of mind (426/2007, p. 84).

Dostoyevsky and understand giving what is Caesar's to Caesar in the way that it was understood in the New Testament?

My answer to this would be: 'no'. There are political implications of our theory. However, rather than lie in a classical utopia, they lie in the carrier of our two times or Vernunft: in the human being itself. She or he is an end in itself, i.e. a utopia, rather than this applying to a state or anything else outside her or him. This, I believe, is still in line with the ideal of an Open Society as propagated by Popper. As suggested in several of the above case studies, our utopia is the human being stripped of their identity: i.e. independently of gender, age, ethnicity, disability and even of their religious affiliation, as all human beings live both in the here and now and have access to eternity. In that sense, the United Nations (UN), which are based on an abstract idea, i.e. a set of values aiming to unite people – all peoples – and, most of all, based on an ideal of universal human equality, can be seen as a Civitate Dei (although it is clear that some people such as former United States Ambassador to the UN Bolton rather saw it as a means to serve particular interests[66]).

Incidentally, although the UN are a Western-inspired idea of which the origins can be traced back to Kant's idea of a league of nations in 'Perpetual peace' (2008), they have consistently aspired to universality. One of their main concepts, which is of particular interest to us in that we said that the political interest of our theory is based on the human being, are human rights. This is the notion that being human itself entails a set of inalienable entitlements. This set of rights has been articulated in the Universal Declaration of Human Rights (UDHR), which all signatory states have committed to realise and guarantee, not only for their citizens, but for all human beings, although the Declaration is not legally binding. It cannot be invoked by the individual against a state. The pre-

---

[66] In a lecture of April 10, 2006, at the University of Delaware, Bolton said: "I think most Americans look at the U.N. from a very and typically pragmatic American point of view ... We don't look at it through ideological lenses. We don't look at it as a perfect institution. We look at it pragmatically and say, 'Can the United Nations solve the international problems to which it's addressed? And if it can't solve those problems, can we fix them? And if we can't fix it, is there something else that we should be using instead?'"

paratory work for this was done by a UNESCO Special Commission established in 1947, which sent a questionnaire to several intellectuals, including Mahatma Gandhi. Gandhi rejected this concept, indicating that there could be no rights without duties. The UDHR passed the UN General Assembly in 1948.

Naturally, from its inception, this document has invoked controversy. The Declaration emphasises political human rights, such as the right to freely express one's opinion, whereas the Government of China for example indicated that safeguarding the survival of its citizens (e.g. being able to provide its population with food) has a higher priority.[67] As such, the Declaration was criticised as being Western, that is, as safeguarding rights that are relevant in a Western situation, where basic needs are met, but not necessarily in other contexts. Human rights also gave rise to some controversy in the Arab world. One article that has been under scrutiny is that referring to the freedom of religion (Art. 18 UDHR). In Islam it is, in principle, not allowed to abandon the religion and apostates may be subjected to capital punishment, which diverges from human rights as per the UDHR. The Norwegian philosopher Jostein Gaardner called for a universal declaration of human obligations (2007), aiming to 'save the planet' from climate change. The idea that the Declaration does not call on duties at all is, however, incorrect. In Art. 29.1, it says: "Everyone has duties to the community in which alone the free and full development of his personality is possible".

The UDHR seems based on the ideals of the French revolution, including freedom and equality. In religions, however, equality is at times a challenge as, they *de facto* follow Durkheim's idea of differentiating between the sacred and the profane; in Israel, Christians, Muslims and other non-Jews may not be considered fully equal to Jews. In Islam, different duties are imposed on non-Muslims than on Muslims. In Christianity, the inequality between Christians and non-Christians seems less

---

[67] A Chinese government white paper 'Human rights in China' (November 1991), probably in reaction to the 1989 unrest, outlined the Chinese standpoint that social turmoil – a possible side-effect of an increased emphasis of individual rights such as freedom – could risk the people's most important collective right, i.e. the right to subsistence.

explicit: in Luke 10:25 – 37, Jesus recounted the parable of the Merciful Samaritan. This Samaritan helped a Jewish traveller, who had become unwell while travelling, regardless of the animosity between Jews and Samaritans at the time, while other Jewish travellers ignored him. Its morale seems to be that values such as mercy and compassion must be upheld independently of the religion of others. Incidentally, the story of the Merciful Samaritan may reflect the culture of the people of the Mashreq region (Jordan, Syria, Palestine, Lebanon and Iraq), which is known as exceptionally hospitable. This hospitability, it is sometimes said, is based on the 'code of the desert': a product of life in harsh desert conditions, where one should assist others for survival, so that, in other circumstances, one can also rely on the assistance of others. In this context, it is ironic to note that, according to the Qur'an, the 'desert Arabs' (i.e. the Bedouins) are the most persistent in their unbelief, see Sura At Tawbah (9), Aya 97.

The philosophical idea behind placing great importance on the individual is that everything else will follow if we care for the human being as a being with intrinsic value. This would mean, in practice, educate him or her according to one's right to education; respect their basic dignity; and, in general, create the conditions for an open society, including a free press. This suggests popular rule, that is to say, democracy. But what does this mean? What is the difference between this and anarchy? I argue that the most precise answer to this question has been given by Immanuel Kant (1784) in his well-known treatise 'What is Enlightenment?' In this, he contended that enlightenment (and, in my interpretation, democracy), consists of two elements: to reason as much as one wants, but obey the king. Michel Foucault examined this answer in an article with the same title, of his own (1984), remarking that it was, in principle, an unexpected answer. The idea that one has of Enlightenment is usually that of an emancipation from Nature, or rather, of replacing superstition (rather than religion) with reason. Obedience would seem to suggest slavery and not generally be perceived to represent one of the pillars of the Enlightenment.

Foucault, however, pointed out that the second element is as much part of Enlightenment as the first: the gist of his discourse seems to be that to reason refers to the rights of the invidual. However, on one's own, a human being can not accomplish anything that would be 'superhuman'. To realise the great works of humanity, those that elevate us above animals, such as the Eiffel Tower, the Great Wall of China, the Pyramids or the Parthenon, human beings have had to work together, subjected as an individual to the collective. This collective can not materialise itself in an uncoordinated manner. The abstract idea, any design, has to be agreed on for it to be possible to focus individual efforts in such a way that they are coordinated with others, and work together towards the same objective. It is this reality that the imperative to obey refers to: one can reason as much as one wants, as this can contribute to the improvement of a design; however, once this is decided upon, one should obey. Whereas reason is the mind of Enlightenment, obedience is its arm. They are interdependent upon one another. In a way, reason represents the here and now and obedience, eternity.

Here we see the difference between democracy, tyranny and anarchy emerge: tyranny is obedience without reason; anarchy reason without obedience; and democracy both reason and obedience. Thus, 'What is Enlightenment?' can be read as a comment on the relation between the individual and the collective, which is itself key to the UDHR. For Enlightenment, free reason may be a necessary condition, but it is not a sufficient one. This interpretation is, of course, optimistic. Horkheimer and Adorno saw an intrinsic tension in the Enlightenment project. While Reason is, on the one hand, considered desirable in that it provides a common ground for carriers of Vernunft (as we discussed earlier on, Descartes thought that shared ideas, based in Reason, could help ensure peace), Horkheimer and Adorno argued that it is also the faculty enabling calculated thinking and, therefore, a force that pits different interests against one another, which may prevail through their effective use of reason (1944/2007, p. 97). Al Ghazali?

This implication of our theory – the central importance of the human being, rather than a utopia – pertaining to political life seems familiar to a specific strand of Judaism, i.e. Reform Judaism, which places emphasis on the importance of the individual. In this case, of course, we emphasise the importance of all individuals, carriers of two times, rather than only persons with a Jewish background. There may also be a connection of this idea with Islam. Brandsma, for example, distinguished between truth (*verité*) and truthfulness (*sincerité*) in an effort to identify a main source of misunderstanding between Muslims and Christians: according to him, for secularists, and for Christians, truth is the most important value of the two, while, for Muslims, it is truthfulness (2006, p. 101). Of course, truthfulness places the individual in the centre. This view may strongly resemble a generic humanism. This may indeed be the case, I do not deny it, but we can call this a religious humanism, as it should be added that it recognises the existence of Deity as the constitution of ourselves, in the time of eternity.

The intuition of the arts

Let us now recapitulate: we discussed that we believe that the essence of being human lies in an existence in two times, the here and now and eternity. While, in consciousness, experience is necessarily limited, focused and therefore fragmented, eternity contains united meaning. As Kant predicted, consciousness is the time-bound translation of eternity and thus of meaning. The intuition of this meaning spells a longing for utopia, for Paradise, which is, in essence, a religious longing. Prophets interrogate this meaning to find solutions to problems in the here and now. There exists, thus, unsurprisingly, a strong intuition of unity under the surface of seemingly random events in everyday life, in many human beings. We can now say that this intuition is probably not coincidental, because we agreed with Plato that intelligence, in essence, consists of the ability to see patterns in seemingly unrelated events. Meaning is the source of reality, which communicates itself through unity's temporal counterpart, the mise en intrigue, which ties events into meaningful 'units'.

The transition from Paradise into the human condition describes a loss of unity: the unity of Nature where everything has its natural and undisputed place, was replaced with an existence in time that is experienced as fragmented reality. It requires Dionysian intoxication to re-experience unity with Nature once again, that is to say, return to Paradise. But intoxication is not the only way: for artist Peter Gabriel, in his song 'Blood of Eden', another way seems to be the unity between a man and a woman. This is reminiscent of Plato's view as told in a myth in 'Symposium', of how the original human beings were split into two (4th century BCE/1995b, pp. 33-35): in this story, one character who sits at a banquet (the *symposion* or feast), tells how the original human being became so strong that they felt confident enough to challenge the Greek gods. They attacked the pantheon on Mount Olympus but were defeated after an ardent battle. To avoid that humans could ever challenge the gods again, they split them in two: men into two men; women into two women; and 'androgynes' (apparently the largest group) into a man and a woman. These partners would from then on always long for one another, never feeling complete on their own. As an act of mercy, the gods would give humans a possibility of temporary relief from their condition via sexual intercourse.

I argue that there exists yet another way to re-establish 'original' unity (which, as discussed before, I do not believe ever existed in the past but is rather a memory of the future), i.e. the unity of here and now and eternity: art, which Camus once called the transcendence of the human being in relation to him- or herself (1942-1945/2013, p. 113). It seems that art has the specific quality or ability to give an idea of what paradise looks and sounds like; artists like, for example, The Beatles allegedly said that it is not they who wrote their works – their songs – but that they were metaphysically inspired. For the Greeks, inspiration came from a muse. And Nietzsche, who asked whether art was a necessary correlate with science (1872/1953, p. 91) defined as the 'mysterious teaching of tragedy':

> [T]he fundamental recognition of the unity of all that exists, the perception of individuation as the original cause of evil, [but] art as the joyful hope that the spell of individuation can be broken, as the notion of a reconstituted unity (id., p. 67)

The link of works of art with the unconscious is very clear in the works of some of the more modern artists such as Dalí, Kahlo and, in literature, Kafka. Numerous voices speak through the artists or authors; voices that come from a beyond that possibly not only the artist knows. Images come from beyond as well, showing mental landscapes that do not only create something new, but also refer to a reality one may believe to have seen before. They may come from eternity.

To start with painting, references to Eden itself are not uncommon in this medium, as for example in the work of the French-Russian painter Marc Chagall. "The Garden of Eden theme in particular", wrote Malzl (2004, p. 226), "was of great significance to Marc Chagall, and he depicted it numerous times in multiple mediums" to the extent that "Pierre Provoyeur, curator of the Musée National Message Biblique Marc Chagall, describes how Chagall viewed it as his 'mission' to portray the paradisiacal theme in paint, thus becoming 'partners [with poets and musicians] in the quest for a lost Eden.'" The idea that Chagall, as a painter-artist, would partner with artists from other fields, such as music, in restoring a lost Eden seems evident to Malzl through his reading of a poster he had developed for a production of Mozart's Magic Flute by the New York Metropolitan Opera: "The similarity of the poster with Chagall's edenic themes does not appear to be a phenomenon of chance", said Malzl (id., p. 220): "everything points to a deliberate attempt by Chagall to draw parallels between The Magic Flute and the Bible, since he felt that both works shared fundamental principles of goodness and truth. … Thus, Chagall pays homage to two major sources of personal and artistic inspiration whose messages he thought to be harmonious."

Chagall is particularly interesting for our story, not only in light of his roots in Jewish culture, which traditionally rejected the art form of painting, but also because of his awareness of the influence of religion on his work. He may have recognised himself as a prophet according to our definition, in as far as he agreed with "his fellow painter Andre Lhote, who said with special reference to Chagall: 'It is the glory and the misery of the artist's lot to transmit a message of which he does not possess the translation.'" (Johnson Sweeney, 1946, p. 7 in Unknown, 1978).

This may not be too surprising for an artist who said that: "The style has no importance. The thing is to express oneself. Painting should have a psychical content" (Sorlier, 1979, p. 54 in Malzl, 2004, p. 221). Given the central importance of time in our theory, it may not be a coincidence that in the work of yet another painter, Dalí, which is particularly surrealistic, the clock, measurement instrument of time, is ubiquitous. It is often a melting clock, an image that seems to refer to the relativity of time upon alteration of modes of consciousness (1935, p. 25). Incidentally, Dalí is said to have met Freud.

It is striking that painting shifted from realistic or figurative to impressionistic not long after photography was developed, making realistic painting redundant. The year 1839 is widely seen as that of the invention of photography and, in the 1860s, impressionism took hold. This is, of course, a simplification: the romantic tradition of painting of the earlier 19th century already valued a style that was less precise (Eco, 2010, p. 308) than that of earlier periods. From that time onward, in painting – that is to say, in the visual arts – something else seems to have happened that reflects that seemingly decisive, consciousness–altering 19th century (of Darwin, of the Industrial Revolution, of technological advances, of Marx, of Nietzsche and, in part, also that of Freud): painting did not just not show empirical reality anymore but just like, according to Foucault, humanity emerged in the sciences (i.e. psychology and cultural anthropology, see earlier discussion), so did it in the arts. To illustrate, Foucault used the famous painting Las Meninas (1656), by Velázquez, in which the painter himself appears. This intuition foreshadowed, according to Foucault, the self-discovery of the human being in the social sciences.

That is, painting started to refer to the human mind rather than all that lie outside of it: like the natural sciences believed that they referred to nature, and we discovered that they referred to nature *and* the concepts that are used to incorporate nature as a system, painting stopped referring to nature only and expressly allowed the human being as its interpreting agent; it began to allow for the lens. And this lens made painting a largely inward-looking affair. Or, as Louise Johnstone wrote in the foreword to a catalogue of an exhibition by painter Claire Harkness, St. Kilda: "accuracy is not the same as truth, and the kind of knowledge elicited through an intuitive and imaginative study can reveal deeper truths about the spirit of a place than any quasi-scientific approach can hope to achieve" (2007, p. unknown). In a few words: painting could become subjective.

Paraphrasing Kwa, whereas, earlier on, the human being was one of the objects to be painted, now he / she became, in addition to that, the painter; or, inversely, whereas first human beings were the painters, she / he also became the painted. This link between nature and art can not only be seen on Velázquez' painting of Las Meninas, or in Meijer's treatise on the classification of art works in museums, where they seemed to be classified as if they were objects from natural history, but also in Nietzsche's idea that nature is the real artist (1872/1953, pp. 32, 39, 41). It might not be a coincidence that it is mostly art, which refers to its own practice as that of 'creation', that changes thoroughly in the 19th century, when in France we observe the ascent of impressionism, as mentioned earlier, and in Germany the rudimentary beginnings of expressionism, which would develop further in the early 20th century. It seems that, from the 19th century onward, painting became enabled to depict eternity in addition to the here and now.

In this respect, the artist plays a role of Prophet similar to that of the intellectual, more so when she or he engages with current social issues. Like the intellectual, and possibly in a more direct and tangible way, the artist functions as an intermediary between this world and the next. The artist's intuition also seems present in contemporary art, including music. For example, the Scottish band Simple Minds named one of their albums 'Good News from the Next World'. The good news, here, refers to the gospels, *eu angelion* (from the Greek εὐαγγέλιον), or evangel, while the next world denotes the origin of the gospels, our eternity. This seems to be aligned with our above analysis, but one wonders to what extent the title was chosen intuitively rather than consciously. But maybe this question is of no importance. After all, as Edith Stein said, there hardly exists a more mysterious spiritual process than how the artist 'conceives' his ideas ... in a manner that is largely hidden from us" (2009, p. 61), that is to say, unconsciously.

In this regard, Plato was wrong when he said that art – theatre – is false (Saint Augustine, 426/2007, p. 106) and in particular forbidden to the guardians of the City State (4th century BCE/1995a, pp. 68). However, it is also difficult to say that (all) art is 'true'; Schelling would even say that art starts where knowledge ends (in: Horkheimer and Adorno, p. 32). The question to what extent artistic expressions should have more latitude than non-artistic ones (a question that became acutely relevant due to artistic expressions implicitly or explicitly criticising the Catholic Church or Islam[68]) are allowed, intertwines art with ethics. In this context, the singer Madonna and her call for artistic freedom of expression in the 1980s and 1990s comes to mind. She asked for a freedom to do what others might find offensive. A religious collective in the Netherlands that felt offended by her performance tried to have her concerts banned. This fits within a tradition of social criticism in the arts. While examples such as that of Madonna show that there may be a fine line, Schopenhauer argued that, while good will is everything in morals, it is nothing in art (1818/1996, II, p. 495). And according to Kant, what is good or bad morally lies in its intention (1785/1996, p. 34) – but, indeed, a good intention may not be sufficient to result in good art.

Plato's consideration has naturally to be seen against the background of his time: in theatres, in his time, actors could ridicule and vent ideas without any accountability. They could say what they wanted, without need for justification. As a result, presumably following the cheer of the audience, or adapting to what they would believe the audience would like, they may at times have resorted to offensive utterances. Saint Augustine strongly criticised the actors of his time as well, suggesting they were vulgar and scandalous, but not for the same reason as Plato: rather, for adhering to allegedly non-existing gods (426/2007, p. 106-107). Plato could not tolerate that theatre or art considered itself to be above scientific scrutiny. That he was not against music as such is shown in his Republic, where one of the classes of society, the guardians, should receive training in harmony; but, interestingly, not all types of music (or musical keys and rhythms) were allowed. The more intox-

---

[68] For example, the Danish cartoon affair.

icating or 'extatic', let's say, Dionysian variations of music were banned from the Republic (4th century BCE/1995a, p. 71) as they could lead the youth astray, which sounds contemporary.[69]

Plato's rejection of the destabilising and, in his view, debilitating force of some arts is reminiscent of Islam's prohibition of dance. As in Christianity, in Islam, adultery is strictly forbidden, and dance is regarded as one of the arts that are thought to be intoxicating to the extent that the human will can no longer prevail and that so the doors to sin, or what to this religion is a sin, are opened. This aligns, to an extent, with Nietzsche's view that music was the most Dionysian of arts, i.e. the most intoxicating one (1872/1953, p. 42). Similarly, Schopenhauer argued that music is the deepest of all arts, as it expresses the inner essence of all life and being (1818/1996, II, p. 522) or even will itself (id., I, p. 359). In the sense of the above, that is, the sense in which art has the function to re-establish for the fragmented human mind the original unity represented in Paradise, music is art *par excellence*. The meditative properties of the Qur'an, of which the verses are often sung, are well-known. However, even though dancing – such as belly-dancing – is not allowed in mainstream Islam, as briefly mentioned above (although this is not stated explicitly in the Qur'an), the dancing *Derwishes*, which belong to a Sufi mystic sect, dance to reach a meditative trance, which is similar to that achieved in prayer, and considered a religious experience.

As to cinema, according to Horkheimer and Adorno (1944/2007), cinema and radio do no longer need to pretend to be art forms. "The truth that they are nothing but commerce is used by them as ideology, which should legitimise the garbage that they purposefully produce", they said (p. 135). Movies, which allow for an almost immediate view of how they will end (p. 139) tend to be made in such a way that they do not permit thought, if one does not want to miss the movie itself (p. 140). Importantly: who is amused consents (p. 159) to this manipulation, where conflicts almost never represent artistic divergences, but almost always diverging political interests (p. 143). While not now intending to

---

[69] In a similar fashion, Plato's observation that, in the past, everything used to better, is often used to illustrate that, essentially, some things seem to be of all times.

examine this issue in-depth, it seems reasonable to postulate the existence and it would probably be possible to describe the outlines of a 'Hollywood ethic', which represent a 'good' and an 'evil' that hypothetically serves political, rather than artistic interests.

The above analysis may, to an extent, clarify the relation between reason and revelation: revelation comes from intuition and, in that respect, speaks of greater truths than reason does. However, reason has to follow revelation, examine it, to ascertain its value. Reason and revelation thus stand to each other as consciousness to unconsciousness, and the here and now to eternity. The revelation appears to experience, and it can challenge and guide reason, like a hypothesis, but it cannot exist only by itself. Reason has to bring it into the human realm, which is consciousness. The above reflection could also help explain why there exists such a great potential for people to appreciate one another's arts across borders, cultures and languages and, by way of speculation, even why some 'ethnic' decorations seem to have similar patterns worldwide: because the inspiration for these different patterns comes from the same eternity. It would, finally, also help to understand to a greater extent the idea of World Heritage.

While intelligence, as argued earlier on, is the ability to see unity in manifoldness, it is not the rejection of manifoldness. It does not mean that the way peoples dress or eat or paint or sing have to be the same everywhere – it only suggests that we have to recognise that these are all expressions of the same human spirit. Probably not all art (a word that, in German, means 'way of doing things') is equally true in the sense of being reflective of eternity and no culture as a whole is superior to any other either. It is well-understood that cultures are largely a response to specific, local circumstances (including, incidentally, the way Arabic women and men dress, which has become, in some instances, a sort of 'Islamic gear').

Both in theory and practice, Plato's notion of unity behind manifoldness is applicable to religion: intelligence helps us see what different religions have in common, not in the sense of an inventory of rules or regulations, but in their essence, namely in ideas underpinning them. Saying this implies accepting that there is a greater truth that can be expressed in several ways, including artistically, similar to what was said about values and norms earlier. In Edith Stein's words (2009, p. 73): "Thomas sees them [ideal objects] as compatible with his teaching on God because he defines the one simple divine essence with the many ideas and explains their plurality as a relation of the divine essence to the many creatures, actual and possible, all resembling the one essence in different ways".

Back to self: transcending identities

As we have now largely addressed the issues we set out to address in this work, i.e. explain my theory of existence in two times and what this means for our interpretation of main religious texts and understandings, there is one cardinal question left to discuss: does Deity exist? How can we understand Deity, if at all? And how can we understand ourselves in relation to Deity? To address these cardinal questions, we need to turn one more time to what Foucault has had to say about time. As mentioned, Foucault essentially described the discovery of the human being in the sciences along with the birth of the historical perspective. This had not always existed in the same form, throughout history. If we look at medieval paintings of the birth of Jesus, for example, we see a setting that often reflects the medieval *Zeitgeist* in terms of dress.

This is so, Foucault thought, because up until a certain period in history, time did not exist. The world was not thought of as developing according to historical periods, but created, at a certain point in time or at different points in time, as Georges Cuvier thought (1813). Little did one know of past stages of development, at that time, as disciplines such as archaeology did hardly exist and, as such, there was no imagination of real progress or growth over time. Foucault's basic thesis was that the way in which we conceptualise time determines the way that we think in general. This is entirely in line with our emphasis on the importance of time for understanding our human condition: that our human condition is determined by living in two times and the idea that time and consciousness equate with one another. In other words: Darwin's theory of evolution changed the way we think about time, and therefore, the way in which we think in general. In that way, Foucault said, we entered a new *episteme*:[70] that of evolution. The previous one had been that of natural history, with its taxonomies, of Linnaeus, primarily, where time, development, does not play a role, except as the theatre stage for a pre-existing truth revealing itself to the observers.

As said before, the new epistème that Foucault described has enabled the establishment of the human sciences and, what is more, it does not only concern the human sciences but also the natural sciences. That is to say, there are underlying structures that play a role across all the sciences, and therefore in processes, in ways of thinking in general, be they political or biological, that can be called epistemic. In the case of Darwin's evolution theory, the notion of the survival of the fittest is an example that influenced thinking far beyond biology, even though, in strict rigour, this was coined by the economist Herbert Spencer and Darwin himself did not support it. The attempts to explain human religious inclinations via evolution theory illustrates just how strong this epistème still is.

Biology is not a human science. It says, to express this in existentialist vocabulary, something about human existence, not about our essence. The human sciences, on the other hand, say something about our essence but, as discussed before, to do so they seem to need an 'Other' that serves as a mirror: in cultural anthropology, other cultures; in psychology, the unconsciousness. In these and other cases, the presupposition, tacit or not, is that somehow these others tell us something about ourselves. If this seems to be mysterious, it is only superficially so. How is it possible that only through the construction of another can we study ourselves? The reason for this would seem to be that, otherwise, the subject and object (the 'I' and the 'it') coincide, leading to a practical

---

[70] Foucault's epistème has been compared with Kuhn's paradigm, and does indeed have similarities with this but is different in that whereas the paradigm concerns one specific academic discipline, the epistème spans the entire academic corpus.

impossibility. Constructing an Other creates a space between the self and this other, and thus an external point of reference that can, as it were, be temporarily inhabited to assess the discrepancies between that other and the position of the subject itself. Just like, for example, we can only see our planet from space, as a planet, but not from Earth itself.

Similarly, it is when one travels that one finds oneself and discovers one's own peculiarities, which may be culturally defined, because in one's own natural environment they disappear into the anonymity of the general. One travels, therefore, not only to find the culture of others, but also one's own, and eventually, hopefully (or not) oneself (a variant of this model that is popular in the internationalisation of education, is the encounter with an Other in one's own culture, or internationalisation at home). We can say that the natural sciences are the sciences of the perceived, while the human sciences are that of the perceiver. The natural sciences are the sciences of perception as substance (where the central question is what is perceived), whereas the human sciences are the sciences of perception as a form (where the central question is how a substance is perceived), thereby mimicking the *doublure* that Foucault described in The Order of Things. This divide seems similar to that between *a priori* and *a posteriori* knowledge as discovered by Kant and to the subjective and objective. The issue with the exponents of the natural sciences that say that the existence of Deity is a question that they can answer is that, to them, the perceiver and her or his a priori knowledge does not (yet) exist. They seem like those that Schopenhauer 1818/1996, II, p. 493) referred to when he spoke of the type of person who:

... nimmt die Dinge in der Welt da, aber nicht die Welt; sein eigenes Tun und Leiden, aber nicht sich.

... perceives the things in the world, but not the world itself; its own acting and suffering, but not her- or himself.

My contention is that, since the diffusion of Darwin's evolution theory there has been another epistemic change that has not only changed perspectives, literally, in the natural sciences, but also in the human sciences and politics: that of relativity theory and, more precisely, Einstein's theory of special relativity. According to this theory, there is no privileged position or 'coordinate system' to describe movement (such as, for example, the trajectory of a stone thrown out of the window of a train in motion). The movement trajectory depends on the position of the observer.

Returning to our initial thought that we can read religious texts on different levels, Foucault's new time and the episteme of relativity have given us the conceptual tools to understand religious texts on a new level. Relativity has underlined the importance of the observer in seeing or understanding truth. There is no one more privileged coordinate system than another, showing the dependence of coordinates on the observer similar to how text depends on its reading. This has opened our eyes to a recursive dimension, that is to say, the ability of the observer to reflect on the observer, or rather of consciousness on consciousness and so, for example, Consciousness Studies. It may not be a coincidence that Horkheimer and Adorno argued that, from a phylo-genetic perspective, i.e. from an evolutionary perspective, self-perception is the most recent acquisition among psychical mechanisms (1944/2007, p. 208), which Bidney (1953) in the manifestation of self-reflection considered uniquely human (in: Dobzhansky, 1969, p. 52).

For religious texts, the additional level that we can add to our understanding relates to the question: who writes? When we say that Deity reveals itself through a text but it is written, or spoken, by Krishna, Moses, Saint Paul or Mohammad, then what does this mean? This means that eternity or the 'other time' in ourselves speaks. Or: might be speaking. Because only if we can reconcile this revelation with reason can we be relatively certain that it is a 'true' revelation. In addition, it means that, together with eternity, it is Krishna, Moses, Saint Paul and Mohammad who write, because they are writing for their time and place (the here and now), that is to say, *from* eternity, but not *for* eternity. This suggests that Deity is an 'Other', in as far as we identify ourselves with the here and now of consciousness and see eternity as a different realm that we venture into from the point of view of our consciousness. This is understandable to the extent that our consciousness is, or at least seems to be, correlated with our individuality – the I in front of the Deity or, as Buber would say, Thou (1923/1937).

But is this really true? In the described model (see Fig. 1), our Creator, communicating Himself to us as meaning is posited at the bottom of the psyche. Should this not be the other way around, in that we have to say that what is divine in humanity is our consciousness? Is this not our really inexplicable element? After all, while it may not be certain to what extent our living companions, animals, are conscious beings, it does seem plausible that the place where we hope to find Deity – namely, in eternity – is only accessible to us in as far as we are conscious. So, in parallel with the discovery of the new, relativistic episteme, should we then not also make the observer visible as, without this observer, revelation would not be possible? There is much that speaks for this. For example, when Adam and Eve ate from the tree of knowledge in the Garden of Eden, they did so because they hoped to become like a Deity. It was then that they were ejected out of eternity, albeit not entirely, as we know now, and entered the here and now. By making this first choice they entered a world where they would have to make choices continuously and where the 'escape from freedom', to use Fromm's phrase, became complicated. This is in line with a passage in the Bible, which says that we are created in God's image (Genesis 1:27).

While I intend to only give a preliminary answer to this question, I would like to emphasise that this view does not only align with our own idea that the human condition is neither only here and now or in eternity; or Buber's idea that the relation with Deity is, or can be, an I – Thou relationship; but also with a highly intricate piece of speculative theology from the German-American philosopher Hans Jonas, born in Mönchengladbach, who developed this in an attempt to understand a great evil while attempting to maintain a belief in meaning, in 'The concept of God after Auschwitz'. Is the idea that God, at the beginning of time, split up into all His beings; that all of us, human beings, together, are our Creator – that God gave Himself, as it were, to time and space, which is to say, consciousness, and so gave up His omnipotence. In this work (1999, p. 134), Jonas wrote:

Im Anfang (...) entschied der göttliche Grund des Seins, sich dem Zufall (...) hinzugeben. Und zwar gänzlich: Da sie einging in das Abenteuer von Raum und Zeit, hielt die Gottheit nichts von sich zurück (...). Damit Welt sei, und für sich selbst sei, entsagte Gott seinem eigenen Sein; er entkleidete sich seiner Gottheit, um sie zurückzuempfangen von der Odyssee der Zeit, beladen mit der Zufallsernte unvorhersehbarer zeitlicher Erfahrung, verklärt oder vielleicht auch entstellt durch sie. (...) Jeder Artenunterschied, den die Evolution hervorbringt, fügt den Möglichkeiten von Fühlen und Tun die eigene hinzu und bereichert damit die Selbsterfahrung des göttlichen Grundes. (...) Die Schöpfung war der Akt der absoluten Souveränität, mit dem sie [Anmerkung: die Gottheit] um des Daseins selbstbestimmter Endlichkeit willen einwilligte, nicht länger absolut zu sein - ein Akt also der göttlichen Selbstentäußerung. (...) Nachdem er sich ganz in die werdende Welt hineingab, hat Gott nichts mehr zu geben: Jetzt ist es am Menschen, ihm zu geben.

In the beginning ... the divine ground of being decided to deliver itself ... to chance. And it did so entirely: as she entered the adventure of space and time, Deity did not hold back in any way. So that the world could exist, and exist for itself, Deity renounced its own existence; it threw off its divinity in order to receive it back from the Odyssey of time, charged with the harvest of coincidence of unpredictable experience in time, enlightened but possibly also disfigured by it. Any difference among species, produced by evolution, adds to the possibilities of feeling and acting its own and with that, enriches the self-experience of the divine ground of being. Creation was an act of absolute sovereignty to which Deity consented so that self-determining finiteness could exist, to no longer be absolute – an act of self-externalisation ... . After God gave Himself entirely to the becoming world, He has nothing left to give anymore: now it is up to the human, to give to Him.

A comparable idea was expressed, later, in a poem by Luc Gorrebeek:

Wachten op een wonder (Waiting for a Miracle). This reads as follows:

> I have heard that many of you are waiting for a miracle; a miracle that I, God, will save the earth
>
> But how will I save without your hands? How will I speak justice without your voice? How will I love without your heart?
>
> From the seventh day, I have given everything out of my hands; all my creation and power to do miracles
>
> Not you, but I am now waiting for the miracle

In a passage in a personal letter of 1956, Carl Jung (1976, p. 311) seems to have pointed at a slightly different, but comparable idea:

> Yahweh's amorality or notorious injustice changes only with the Incarnation into the exclusive goodness of God. This transformation is connected with his becoming man and therefore exists only if it is made real through the conscious fulfilment of God's will in man. If this realization does not occur, not only the Creator's amorality is revealed but also his unconsciousness. With no human consciousness to reflect themselves in, good and evil simply happen, or rather, there is no good and evil, but only a sequence of neutral events ...

Certainly, like almost any philosophical, theological or other thought, this idea reflects only a part of the truth, if at all as, in practice, and seemingly, we can never fully be eternity whilst existing as individuals. In that sense, eternity will, for a considerable time to come, remain a mysterious other. But it does seem to be true that, while as individual human beings we are caged in by our conditioned, fragmented existence in the here and now, subject to the cycle of life, collectively, life is not mortal and is capable of creating an in principle infinite number of 'here and now's'. Therefore while, for the individual, Deity will remain an 'Other' in the depths of our minds, only in as far as individuals converge in eternity, if someone were to ask whether Deity exists, we might respond: yes, we exist.

Bibliography

References not included in this list include the Bible, the Qur'an and the Universal Declaration of Human Rights.

If not otherwise indicated, translations from other languages into English, in quotations, are by the author.

Achterhuis, H. (1969). *Camus: De moed om mens te zijn* (Camus: The courage to be human). Utrecht: Ambo.

Agamben, G. (2003). *Das Offene: der Mensch und das Tier* (The open: the human being and the animal). Frankfurt am Main: Suhrkamp.

Ali, T. (2003). *The clash of fundamentalisms*. London: Verso.

Alighieri, D. (2008). *De goddelijke komedie*. Amsterdam: Athenaeum – Polak & Van Gennep. (Originally 1320)

Arens, K. (1989). *Structures of knowing*. Dordrecht / Boston / London: Kluwer Academic Publishers.

Aristophanes (1957). *Plays II. Lysistrata*. Transl. Patric Dickinson. London: Oxford University press. (Originally 411 BCE)

Augustinus, A. (2007). *De stad van God* (The city of God). Amsterdam: Ambo. (Originally 426)

Augustine, A. (1995). *Belijdenissen* (Confessions). 1995. Transl. G. Wijdeveld. Amsterdam: Athenaeum / Polak & Van Gennep. (Originally 400)

Avineri, S. (1981). *The making of modern Zionism*. New York: Basic Books.

Bacon, F. (1985). *The essays*. London: Penguin. (Originally 1597)

Benthem, J. Van. (2000). *Information is the only resource that grows with use* (motto). In: Institute for Logic, Language and Computation. Logic in action 1999. Amsterdam: ILLC.

Berlin, I. (1970). *Four essays on liberty*. London: Oxford University press.

Bilagher, M. (2005). What is qualitative research? *UNRWA Student/Teacher Journal*, Nrs. 1 and 2, June and December, 8-13.

Bilagher, M. (2006). *Wetenschap en religie: waar is het conflict?* In: Gamma. Jrg. 13, nr. 4, December.

Bilagher, M. (2008). *From Absolute Mind to zombie: Is artificial intelligence possible?* Essay for G.D. & M.C. Harris Prize of Kellogg College, University of Oxford. Unpublished.

Bilagher, M. (2010). The Prophet as Intellectual and Vice Versa: A Psychoanalytical Interpretation of the Phenomenon of Prophecy. *Time & Mind*, Vol. 3, Nr. 1, pp. 63-83.

Bloom, B.S. [and 33 others] (1984). *Taxonomy of educational objectives: Book 1 cognitive domain*. New York, NY: Longman. (Originally 1956)

Bos, A-.M. (1996). *Democratie en rechtsstaat*. Nijmegen: Ars Aequi Libri.

Brandsma, B. (2006). *De hel, dat is de ander* (The hell, that is the other). Diemen: Veen.

Brinton, C. (1953). *The Shaping of the Modern Mind*. New York: New American Library.

Buber, M. (1937). *I and Thou*. Edinburgh: T. & T. Clark. (Originally 1923)

Buber, M. (1972). *Paden in Utopia* (Paths in Utopia). Utrecht: Bijleveld.

Campbell, J. (1998). *The power of myth*. Interview by: Bill Moyers. Betty Sue Flowers (Ed.). New York: Doubleday.

Camus, A. (2013). *Carnets II*. Paris: Gallimard. (Originally 1942-1945)

Chalmers, D. (1995). Facing up to the problem of consciousness. *Journal of Consciousness Studies*, 2, 3, pp. 200 – 219.

Government of China (1991). *Human rights in China*. White paper. Retrieved 7 January 2019 from: http://www.chinaembassy.lt/eng/zt/zfbps/t125236.htm

Cliteur, P. (2001). *Darwin, dier en recht*. Amsterdam: Boom.

Cohen, A. (2021). *Il Talmud*. Bari-Roma: Gius. Laterza & Figli Spa. (Originally 1921)

Cohen, R. (2007). Gaining political clout of Biblical proportions? *International Herald Tribune*, 10 - 11 February.

Cohn-Sherbok, D. (2007). *Fifty key Jewish thinkers*. New York / London: Routledge.

Confucius (1979). *The analects*. Harmondsworth / New York: Penguin Books. (Originally 3rd Century BCE)

Crotty, M. (1998). *The foundations of social research: Meaning and perspective.* 1998. London: Sage publications.

Cusanus, N. (1954). *Of learned ignorance.* Transl. Fr. Germain Heron. London: Routledge & Kegan Paul. (Originally 1440)

Cusanus, N. (1993). *Het zien van God / De visione Dei* (The vision of God). Kampen: Kok Agora. (Originally 1453)

Cuvier, M. (1813). *Essay on the theory of the earth.* Translation by Robert Kerr. Edinburgh: William Blackwood.

Dalí, S. (1935). *La Conquête de l'irrationnel.* Paris: Éditions surréalistes.

Darwin, C. (1958). *The autobiography of Charles Darwin 1809 - 1882.* [With original omissions restored. Edited with Appendix and Notes by his grand-daughter Nora Ballow.]. London: Collins.

Darwin, C. (1994). *The correspondence of Charles Darwin.* Volume 9. 1861. Cambridge: Cambridge University Press.

Dawkins, R. (2007). *The God delusion.* London: Transworld.

Descartes, R. (1972). *Treatise of man.* Translation and commentary by Thomas Steele Hall. Cambridge, Massachusetts: Harvard University Press. (Originally 1633)

Descartes, R. (2008). *A discourse on the method.* Translation by Ian Maclean. Oxford: Oxford University Press. (Originally 1637)

Dewey, J. (2011). *Democracy & education.* Mansfield Center, CT: Martino Publishing. (Originally 1916)

Dobzhansky, T. (1969). *The biology of ultimate concern.* London: Rapp & Whiting.

Dostoyevsky, F. (1958). *De gebroeders Karamazow* (The brothers Karamazow). 1992. Transl. J. van der Eng. Amsterdam: G.A. van Oorschot.

Durkheim, E. (2008). *The elementary forms of religious life.* Oxford: Oxford University Press. (Originally published 1912)

Eco, U. (1999). *De slinger van Foucault* (Foucault's pendulum). 1999. Amsterdam: Bert Bakker.

Eco, U. (2010). *On beauty.* London: Quercus - Maclehouse Press.

Einstein, A. Ernst Mach. 1916. In: *Physikalische Zeitschrift.* Nr. 17

Fabian, J. (1983). *Time and the Other*. New York: Columbia University Press.

Foucault, M. (2005). *The order of things*. London: Routledge. (Originally 1966)

Foucault, M. (1984). Qu'est-ce que les Lumières ? In : *Dits et Ecrits*, Tome IV, pp. 562-578.

Fox, K. (2004). *Watching the English*. London: Hodder & Stoughton.

Fresco, L. (2007). *'Voedsel hoort bij de canon van het dagelijkse bestaan'* ('Food should be regarded as common knowledge'). Interview by R. Hartgers. In: Spui, 2007/1, nr. 23, pp. 4-5.

Freud, S. (1961). *The future of an illusion*. New York & London: W.W. Norton & Company. (Originally 1927)

Freud, S. (1967). *Moses and monotheism*. New York: Vintage Books. (Originally 1939)

Freud, S. (1989). *Opmerkingen over een geval van dwangneurose ('De Rattenman'). Oorspronkelijke notities betreffende de 'Rattenman'*. (Observations on a case of compulsive neurosis ('The rat man'). Original notes pertaining to the 'rat man'. Meppel / Amsterdam: Boom.

Freud, S. (1991). *Zelfportret. De weerstanden tegen de psychoanalyse. Het vraagstuk van de lekenanalyse*. (Self-portrait. The refutations of psychoanalysis. The question of lay analysis). Meppel / Amsterdam: Boom.

Fromm, E. (1984). *The fear of freedom*. London: Routledge Clasics.

Fukuyama, F. (1992). *Het einde van de geschiedenis en de laatste mens* (The end of history and the last man). 1992. Amsterdam: Contact.

Gaardner, J. (2007). *A user's manual for our planet*. In: UNESCO Courier (nr. 9).

Galtung, J. (1964). An editorial. *Journal of Peace Research*, Vol. 1, Nr. 1, pp. 1-4.

Gardner, H. (2011). *Frames of mind: The theory of multiple intelligences*. New York, NY: Basic Books.

Garrett, J. (2004). *Hierarchy Ethics and Enlightenment Ethics*. Website. Retrieved 4 February 2019, from: http://people.wku.edu/jan.garrett/320/hierenlt.htm

Goedegebuure, J. (1986). Het ondenkbare denken (Thinking the unthinkable). In: P. Meeuse (ed.). *Harmonie als tegenspraak* (Harmony as contradiction). Amsterdam: De bezige bij.

Le Goff, J., 1988. *The Medieval Imagination.* Chicago: University of Chicago Press.

Goldberg, D. & Rayner, J. (1989). *The Jewish people: Their history and their religion.* London: Penguin.

Goodman, D. & Russell, C.A. (Eds.). (1991). *The rise of scientific Europe 1500 - 1800.* London: Hodder & Stoughton.

Gorrebeek, L. (Unknown). *Wachten op een wonder* (Waiting for a miracle). Unpublished.

Gould, S.J. (1987). Nonoverlapping magisteria. *Natural history.* Nr. 106, pp. 16-22.

Gur Ze'ev, I. (2000). *Philosophy of peace education in a postmodern era.* Keynote address to International Network of Philosophers of Education biennial conference. Retrieved 22 July 2007, from: http://construct.haifa.ac.il/~ilangz/peace23.html.

Ha'am, A. (1962). *Nationalism and the Jewish ethic.* 1962. New York: No publisher.

Haeckel, E. (1866). *Generelle Morphologie der Organismen: Allgemeine Grundzüge der organischen Formen-Wissenschaft, mechanisch begründet durch die von C. Darwin reformirte Decendenz-Theorie.* Berlin: G. Reimer.

Hakim, C. (2010). Erotic capital. *European Sociological Review,* Vol. 26, Iss. 5, pp. 499–518. https://doi.org/10.1093/esr/jcq014

Hedley Brooke, J. (2006). Contributions from the history of science and religion. In: Philip Clayton and Zachary Simpson, editors, *The Oxford Handbook of Science and Religion.* Oxford: Oxford University Press, pp. 193-310.

Heidegger, M. (2006). *Sein und Zeit.* Tübingen: Max Niemeyer Verlag. (Originally 1927)

Heinisch, K.J. (1960). *Der Utopische Staat* (The utopian state). Reinbek bei Hamburg: Rowohlt.

Hendrikse, K. (2006). De atheïstische dominee spreekt. *Trouw* (3 November).

Hirsch, S. (1842). *Die Religions Philosophie der Juden*. 1842. Leipzig: Hunger Verlag.

Holton, G. (1986). *The advancement of science, and its burdens*. Cambridge: Cambridge University Press.

Hooykaas, R. (1976). *Geschiedenis der natuurwetenschappen* (History of the natural sciences). Utrecht: Boon, Scheltema & Holkema.

Hooykaas, R. (1973). *Religion and the rise of modern science*. Edinburgh: Scottish academy press.

Horkheimer, M. & Adorno, T.W. (2007). *Dialectiek van de Verlichting*. Amsterdam: Boom. (Originally 1944)

Hume, D. (1799). *Essays on suicide and the immortality of the soul*. Basel: James Decker.

Huntington, S. (1993). The clash of civilizations? In: *Foreign Affairs*, Summer, pp. 22-49.

Jacobi, J., 1949. *The psychology of Jung*. London: Routledge & Kegan Paul.

Johnson Sweeney, J. (1946). *Marc Chagall*. New York: Museum of Modern Art.

Johnstone, L. (2007). *Foreword to exhibition St. Kilda, by Claire Harkness*. Plockton: Plockton Gallery.

Jonas, H. (1999). *Mortality and morality*. Ed. Lawrence Vogel. Evanston, Illinois: Northwestern university press.

Jung, C.G. (1982). *Psychologie en religie* (Psychology and religion). Rotterdam: Lemniscaat.

Jung, C.G. (1970). *Bewußtes und Unbewußtes*. 1970. Frankfurt am Main: Fischer Bücherei.

Jung, C.G. (1976). *Letters 1951-1961*. Selected & edited by Gerhard Adler in collaboration with Aniela Jaffé. London: Routledge & Kegan Paul.

Kant, I. (1784). Beantwortung der Frage: Was ist Aufklärung? *Berlinischen Monatsschrift*, Dezember. H. 12, pp. 481–494.

Kant, I. (1956). *Kritik der reinen Vernunft* (Critique of pure reason). Hamburg: Felix Meiner Verlag. (Originally 1781)

Kant, I. (1990). *Critique of pure reason*. Amherst: Prometheus books. (Originally 1781)

Kant, I. (1996). *Kritik der praktischen Vernunft.Grundlegung zur Metaphysik der Sitten* (Critique of practical reason. Groundwork of the metaphysics of morals). Frankfurt am Main: Suhrkamp. (Originally 1785)

Kant, I. (2008). *Zum ewigen Frieden* [Perpetual peace]. Stuttgart: Reclam. (Originally 1795)

Heller, K.D. (1964). *Ernst Mach*. Vienna / New York: Springer Verlag.

Kennedy, J. (2002). *Een weloverwogen dood: Euthanasie in Nederland*. Amsterdam: Bert Bakker.

Kroonenberg, S. (2007). *De menselijke maat* (The human measure). Amsterdam / Antwerpen: Atlas.

Kuçuradi, I. (2007). *A Sisyphean task*. 2007. In: UNESCO Courier (nr. 9).

Kuhn, T.S. (1970). *The structure of scientific revolutions*. London: University of Chicago press.

Kwa, C.L. (1991). Wetten en verhalen: Discursieve en narratieve verbeeldingen van de natuur (Laws and stories: Discursive and narrative representations of nature). In: *Kennis en Methode*, Nr. 15, pp. 105–120.

Kwa, C.L. (1992). Épistèmes en paradigma's (Epistemes and paradigms). In : *Kennis en Methode*, Nr. 16, pp. 215–221.

Kwa, C.L. (2005). *De ontdekking van het weten* (The discovery of knowledge). Amsterdam: Boom.

Labrie, A. (1989). *De reis naar Utopia* (The voyage to Utopia). In: Skript historisch tijdschrift. Winter 1989, jaargang 11, nr, 4, pp. 196–212.

Levi, P. (2000). *De getuigenissen. Is dit een mens & Het respijt & De verdronkenen en de geredden* (The confessions. If this is a man & The truce & The drowned and the saved). Amsterdam: Meulenhoff.

Lewis, C.S. (1961). *Dienstanweisungen für einen Unterteufel* (The Screwtape letters). Freiburg im Breisgau: Herder Verlag.

Loo, H. Van der & Reijen, W. Van (1990). *Paradoxen van modernisering* (Paradoxes of modernisation). Muiderberg: Coutinho.

Machiavelli, N. (1998). *De heerser* (The Prince). Amsterdam: Athenaeum – Polak & Van Gennep. (Originally 1532)

Mach, E. (1987). *Analyse der Empfindungen* (Analysis of sensations). 1987. Darmstadt: Wissenschaftliche Buchgesellschaft. (Originally 1922)

Magris, C. (1998). *Microcosmi* (Microcosms). Transl. A. Haakman. Amsterdam: Bert Bakker.

Magris, C. (2001a). *Danube.* London: The Harvill press.

Magris, C. (2001b). *Langs grenzen* (Along broders). Transl. A. Haakman. Introduction W. Otterspeer. Amsterdam: Bert Bakker.

Magris, C. (2018). *Journeying.* New Haven and London: Yale University Press.

Malinowski, B. (1931). Culture. In: E.R.A. Seligman & A. Johnson (Eds.), *Encyclopaedia of the Social Sciences* (Vol. IV). Pp. 621-645 New York: MacMillan.

Malzl, P.B. (2004). An Allegory of Eden: Marc Chagall's Magic Flute Poster. *BYU Studies Quarterly,* Vol. 43, Nr. 3, Art. 17. Retrieved 5 February 2019 from: https://scholarsarchive.byu.edu/cgi/viewcontent.cgi?referer=https://www.google.com/&httpsredir=1&article=4118&context=byusq

Manuel, F. & Manuel, F. (1982). *Utopian thought in the Western world.* Cambridge, Mass.: Belknap / Harvard University Press.

Marcel, G. (1951). *Homo viator: Introduction to the metaphysics of hope.* London: Victor Gollancz.

Marcuse, H. (1975). *De één-dimensionale mens* (One-dimensional man). Bussum: Paul Brand.

McGrath, A. & McGrath, J.C. (2007). *The Dawkins delusion?* Downers Grove, IL: IVP Books.

Meijers, D.J. (1991). *Kunst als natuur* (Art as nature). Amsterdam: SUA.

Meyer, H. (2007). *Onze Joden* (Our Jews). In: EAJG Nieuwsbrief, jaargang 1, nr. 3, July.

More, T. (2001). *Utopia.* New Haven: Yale University press. (Originally 1516)

Mumford, L. (1959). *The story of utopias.* Gloucester Massachusetts: Peter Smith. (Originally 1922)

Naipaul, V.S. (1991). *Our Universal Civilization.* In: New York Review of Books, 31 January 1991, pp. 4-7.

Nietzsche, F. (1953). *Die Geburt der Tragödie aus dem Geiste der Musik* (The birth of tragedy). Stuttgart: Philipp Reclam. (Originally 1872)

Nietzsche, F. (1968a). *Also sprach Zarathustra* (Thus spoke Zarathustra). Berlin: Walter de Gruyter. (Originally 1885)

Nietzsche, F. (1968b). *Jenseits von Gut und Böse. Zur Genealogie der Moral* (Beyond good and evil. The genealogy of morals). Berlin: Walter de Gruyter. (Originally 1887)

Nietzsche, F. (1973). *Die Fröhliche Wissenschaft.* Berlin: De Gruyter. (Originally 1973)

Plato (1995a). *Constitutie.* Politeia (The Republic). Amsterdam: Athenaeum – Polak and Van Gennep. (Originally 4th century BCE)

Plato (1995b). *Sokrates' leven en dood: Feest / Symposium. Euthyfron. Sokrates' verdediging. Kriton. Faidon* (Socrates' life and death: Feast / Symposium. Euthyphro. Apology. Crito. Phaedo). Amsterdam: Athenaeum – Polak & Van Gennep. (Originally 4th century BCE)

Pleticha, H. & Schönberger, O. [publishers] (1980). *Die Römer* (The Romans). Gütersloh: Prisma Verlag.

Popper, K. (1994). *La lezione di questo secolo* (The lesson of this century). Interview with Giancarlo Bossetti. Venezia: Marsilio.

Popper, K. (2003). *The open society and its enemies.* Vol. 2, Hegel and Marx. London: Routledge. Originally 1945.

Popper, K. (2006). *Conjectures and refutations.* London: Routledge. (Originally 1963)

Popper, K. (2019). *The open society and its enemies.* Abingdon & New York: Routledge. (Originally 1945)

Prins, A. (2007). *Verveling als cultuurverschijnsel* (Boredom as a cultural phenomenon). Interview by: M. Meijer. In: Filosofie Magazine, jaargang 16, 05-2007, pp. 26-29.

Ramdas, A. (2004). *Wars van duiding.* In: NRC Handelsblad 22 November 2004.

Ramdas, A. (1993). *In mijn vaders huis* (In my father's house). Amsterdam: Jan Mets.

Ricoeur, P. (1983). *Temps et récit. Tome I* (Time and narrative. Part I). Paris: Éditions du seuil.

Rorty, R. (1980). *Philosophy and the mirror of nature*. Oxford: Basil Blackwell.

Rosenthal-Schneider, I. (1980). *Reality and scientific truth*. 1980. Detroit: Wayne State university press.

Russell, B. (2007). *The history of Western philosophy*. London: Routledge. (Originally 1945)

Sartre, J.-P. (1996). *Existentialism and humanism*. Transl. Philip Mairet. London: Methuen & Co. (Originally 1946)

Sartre, J.-P. (1987). *Huis clos*. London: Methuen Educational. (Originally 1944)

Savorgnan di Brazza, F. (1941). *Da Leonardo a Marconi: Invenzioni e scoperte Italiane* (From Leonardo to Marconi: Italian discoveries and inventions). Milano: Ulrico Hoepli.

Schopenhauer, A. (1996). *Die Welt als Wille und Vorstellung* (The world as will and representation). Frankfurt am Main / Leipzig: Insel Verlag. (Originally 1818)

Selim, N. (2003). *De vrouwen van de profeet*. Amsterdam: Van Gennep.

Sheldrake, R. (1994). *Een nieuwe levenswetenschap* (A new science of life). Utrecht / Antwerpen: Kosmos.

Simpson, J. (2003). An instinct for dragons (book review). *Reviews of Folklore Scholarship*, Vol. 114, Nr. 1, p. 134.

Smith, H. (1991). *The world's religions*. New York: HarperCollins. (Originally published 1958)

Sorlier, S. (1979). *Chagall by Chagall*. New York: Harry N. Abrams.

Stein, E. (2009). *Potency and act*. Washington, DC: ICS Publications.

Spinoza, B. De (1981). *Ethics*. Salzburg: Universität Salzburg, Institut für Anglistik und Amerikanistik.

Tillich, P. (1963). *Systematic Theology*. Vol. III. Chicago: University of Chicago Press.

Tolstoy, L. (2006). *Oorlog en vrede* (War and peace). Amsterdam: G.A. van Oorschot. (Originally 1869)

Toulmin, S. (1990). *Cosmopolis: The hidden agenda of modernity*. Chicago: The university of Chicago press.

Toulmin, S. & Goodfield, J. (1982). *The discovery of time*. Chicago / London: University of Chicago press.

Unknown (1978). *Nine windows by Chagall*. New York: Museum of Modern Art. Retrieved 5 February 2019 from: https://www.moma.org/documents/moma_catalogue_2356_300062542.pdf

Wegter-McNelly, K. (2006). Fundamental physics and religion. In: Philip Clayton and Zachary Simpson, editors, *The Oxford Handbook of Science and Religion*. Oxford: Oxford University Press, pp. 156-171.

Wilson, E.O. (2003). *The future of life*. London: Penguin.

Winter, L. de (2005). *Tolerating a time bomb*. In: New York Times 16 July 2005. Retrieved 15 December 2007 from: http://www.nytimes.com/2005/07/16/opinion/16winter.html.

Wittgenstein, L. (1969). *Tractatus logico-philosophicus*. In: Schriften 1. Frankfurt am Main: Suhrkamp.

Wolters, G. (1987). *Mach I, Mach II, Einstein und die Relativitätstheorie*. 1987. Berlin: Walter de Gruyter.